The Heart of Sicily

The Heart of Sicily

Recipes and Reminiscences of Regaleali
A COUNTRY ESTATE

ANNA TASCA LANZA

Photographs by
FRANCO ZECCHIN

Foreword by
MARY TAYLOR SIMETI

Clarkson Potter/Publishers
New York

Published by Clarkson N. Potter, Inc., 201 East 50th Street, New York, New York 10022.
Member of the Crown Publishing Group.
Random House, Inc. New York, Toronto, London, Sydney, Auckland.
CLARKSON N. POTTER, POTTER and colophon are trademarks of Clarkson N. Potter, Inc.

Manufactured in Japan.

Design by

DONNA AGAJANIAN

Library of Congress Cataloging-in-Publication Data
Lanza, Anna Tasca.
The heart of Sicily : recipes and reminiscences of life at Regaleali, a country estate / Anna Tasca Lanza ; photographs
by Franco Zecchin ; foreword by Mary Taylor Simeti.
Includes index.
1. Regaleali (Sicily)   2. Cookery, Italian—Sicilian style.
3. Cookery—Italy—Sicily.   I. Title.
TX723.2.S55L35   1993
641.5945'8—dc20   92-45598
                                                                                                           CIP

ISBN 0-517-58961-3
10 9 8 7 6 5 4 3 2 1

FRONTISPIECE: *A Madonna at the front door of the Case Grandi.*

For my mother and father,
whose love never leaves me wherever I am.

Contents

Foreword

THE TASCA FAMILY tradition of fine food first came to my notice quite by chance, in an Italian magazine article about the return to fashion of fancy weddings. For the marriage of the count's granddaughter, the article said, the wedding breakfast at Villa Tasca included medallions of chicken served in baskets woven of pasta and decorated with fresh flowers dipped in wax, the re-creation of a centuries-old recipe their chef had discovered in the family archives.

I was researching the history of Sicilian food at the time and longed to know more, but I was far too shy to present myself out of the blue, my natural timidity intensified by the rather daunting picture of the Sicilian aristocracy and its chefs that was emerging from my reading. I had been using the loving descriptions of food in Giuseppe di Lampedusa's novel *The Leopard* to show how the elaborate dishes developed in the baronial kitchens—dishes with roots that went back through the Renaissance as far as the classical era—had been joined in the nineteenth century by newcomers from the north. In the famous ballroom scene, for example, "[h]uge blond *babas, Mont Blancs* snowy with whipped cream" take their place on the refreshment table beside traditional Sicilian sweets such as the "triumph of gluttony" and the "virgins' cakes."

The fashion for French cooking had invaded the Kingdom of the Two Sicilies on the heels of Napoleon's army, and a French-trained chef became a status symbol in Sicily's aristocratic houses. Endowed with great prestige and influence, the *monzù* (a local corruption of "monsieur") added consommé and foie gras to the Sicilian menu and gilded the local culinary lilies with vast quantities of cream and butter.

In the early decades of the twentieth century, Sicily emerged as a favorite winter resort for European royalty, and the Palermo *monzù* chefs cooked for kings and kaisers. One of the most distinguished of these, Giovanni Messina, reigned in the Tasca kitchens for more than half a century, and it was his pupil and heir, Mario Lo Menzo, to whom the magazine article referred. No wonder I was intimidated.

References to the employers tended to be equally discouraging. The men the *monzù* chefs served were passionate about the prestige and quality of their table, but they disdained the practicalities of financing it. Enlightened exceptions notwithstanding, the Sicilian aristocrats were much more preoccupied with spending the income from their

OVERLEAF: *Tombs of prehistoric settlers are carved in the limestone above Regaleali.*

vast agricultural holdings than they were with improving them. Some cultivated with greater success the arts and letters: the hero of *The Leopard* tries to avoid administering his estates by taking refuge in astronomy.

Not all of his peers were that refined. One eighteenth-century baron, eager to impress his feudal domains by arriving with pomp in coach and four but determined not to spend a penny on widening the roads, ordered his coachman to harness the strongest horse to the sturdiest carriage and to drive at full gallop toward the gap in the rocks that obstructed his passage. No lives were lost, but the rocks survived better than the coach.

As far as history is concerned, such anecdotes are as revealing as they are amusing, but I have since discovered that they are not very relevant to the Tasca household. When I finally did interview him, chef Mario proved to be extremely amiable, as generous with his laughter as he is with his recipes, and as I came to know Anna Tasca Lanza, I learned that she is justifiably angered by journalists who describe her father, the present Count of Almerita, as the "last of the Leopards." While he does share Prince Fabrizio's appreciation of fine cooking, Giuseppe Tasca is no resigned witness to aristocratic decline; he is rather a successful farmer and a daring entrepreneur who has transformed the small winery on the family estate of Regaleali into an international concern. His is one of the few private houses still to perpetuate the great Sicilian baronial cuisine, yet he and his family are deeply attached to the rural world of Regaleali, its products, and its traditions.

It is the link with Regaleali that gives a special character both to the history of the Tascas and to their cooking. This vast tract of gently rolling hills in the center of Sicily's wheat-growing interior was purchased in 1830 by the Mastrogiovanni Tasca brothers, rich grain merchants from eastern Sicily. Although their heirs married into the aristocracy, through the generations they have remained dedicated agriculturalists, first turning Regaleali into a model farm by introducing new techniques and price-winning strains of wheat and cattle and then, in recent years, replacing outdated crops with the vineyards that furnish the Regaleali winery.

The food that Anna Lanza presents in the following pages is colored by this double thread of Sicilian history, the aristocratic and the agrarian. It is, as anyone who has had the privilege of eating at Regaleali can testify, exceptionally fine food, prepared for the most part from ingredients produced on the estate: lamb and poultry from the Tasca flocks, ricotta and pecorino from the day's milking, vegetables from the garden, and fruit from the orchards. There are the elaborate showpieces Mario creates for special occasions, and the simple and strongly flavored vegetable dishes that visitors to the island rarely have occasion to taste, since Sicilians consider them too humble to offer to guests.

On Easter Sunday the Tascas expect to eat their lamb in a rich, cream-based fricassee that only a *monzù* would have invented, but as children, Anna relates, they used to squabble among themselves over who got to eat the *Stigghiole*, delicious but decidedly plebeian twists of grilled baby lamb intestines, more commonly sold in the streets and market-places of Palermo. The elemental and earthy tastes of country cooking—sun-dried tomato extract, home-baked bread, *Spaghetti Aglio, Olio, e Peperoncino*—alternate with the sophisticated nuances of a more cosmopolitan cuisine: *Pasta alla Moda dei Monzù*—in which the only typically Sicilian ingredient is the pasta—or Prince of Wales Cheese Brioche.

The recipes follow the dictates of the seasons and their festivals and of the caprices and tastes of strong-minded family members. At Regaleali, as in any kitchen that still has close ties to the land, one prepares what the season provides; feast-day menus were decided upon decades ago. The personal preferences of the count have become Mario's prejudices. Anna and her sisters (all expert cooks) defend their own inclinations, and the countess manages to reconcile everybody before they reach the dinner table. What results is a distinctive and very personal version of Sicilian cooking.

In *The Heart of Sicily* it is Anna's voice that provides the most distinctive flavor of all. Together with her recipes she shares with us her world, in a delightful blend of personal and regional history. She takes us by word and by photograph through a year at Regaleali, showing us how the changing seasons alter both the landscape and the food it produces, describing in a beguiling fashion the rituals with which the Tascas observe their family anniversaries, the feast days of their faith, and the crucial moments of sowing and harvesting. Each page is imbued with her tolerant, amused, but passionate love for Regaleali's past and her profound commitment to preserving and projecting the best of Regaleali into the future. The book is a celebration of family, of the deep and constant affection and respect, and the occasional friction, which bind it, a celebration of the responsibilities and rewards of belonging to a tradition, of having strong roots.

In the preface to my own book on Sicilian cooking, I said that the inspiration to write the book had come from my discovery that Sicily's "density of history and tradition is fascinating and deeply satisfying when it informs and gives substance to the actions and rituals of daily life." It is hard to imagine a better illustration of what I was trying to say than the story of Regaleali and its cooking.

Mary Taylor Simeti
Palermo

The summer I was four.

Introduction

MY FAMILY HOME, Regaleali, is at the very heart of Sicily. Once a vast agricultural estate, it is now primarily a winery, though here we continue to raise sheep for cheese and meat and to grow all our own produce. The first known inhabitants of Regaleali came there in the Bronze Age; they were drawn to the site by a freshwater spring, which still feeds the drinking trough in front of the main house. Our famous spring provides just a trickle these days; each drop is precious.

The tombs of those prehistoric settlers are carved in the limestone above the *masseria* (farm). Traces of Greek and Roman colonization have also been found at Regaleali; in fact, beneath the *masseria* lie remnants of a Roman villa. In Arab times, the place was called Rahal-Ali, or village of Ali, and the name stuck. During the late Middle Ages, it was part of the region of Sclafani, which was governed by powerful feudal lords. The estate passed into my family's hands in the early nineteenth century.

Food preparation at Regaleali follows the time-honored concepts and methods that absorbed the culinary traditions of Sicily's conquerors to create a distinctive culinary tradition with very ancient roots. Sicily, which was at the crossroads of the Mediterranean world, was ruled first by the Greeks; for a time the city of Siracusa on the southern coast of Sicily was the gastronomic capital of the Mediterranean. Sicilian cheese, whether caciocavallo or pecorino, is still made the ancient Greek way. It is a primitive and laborious method, but the cheese is like no other in the world.

The Greeks were followed by the Romans, the Arabs, the Normans, the French, and the Spanish. Monuments of their cultures still stand: massive Greek temples; churches decorated in a mixture of Arab, Greek, and Roman styles; classical architecture; Mediterranean-style roofs and patios.

The Crusaders also passed through Sicily on their way to the Holy Land and Rhodes. The merchants who crisscrossed the Mediterranean made landfall at Sicilian ports, leaving traces of their rich and varied cultures behind. Closer to our own time, American troops landed in Sicily during World War II. Today large numbers of tourists from northern Europe and migrant laborers from North Africa have been drawn to the island in search of sun or work.

All those conquerors and wayfarers have made an imprint on Sicilian cuisine, but without altering its basic character. The main element of Sicilian cooking has always been the sun. Its energy gives Sicilian food its richness and flavor. The grape, from which we get wine and vinegar as well as raisins and dried currants; the olive, source of precious oil; fresh fruits and vegetables; herbs; wheat of the highest quality—all flourish under the Sicilian sun. These ingredients have dominated our table since the beginning of time. Sugarcane, citrus, and rice were introduced by the Arabs; the New World's tomatoes and peppers came much later.

The Romans in their day exploited Sicily as a granary. The island exported hard durum wheat, the best there is, which we still use today for pasta and bread. The fame of Sicilian cuisine spread throughout the classical world, and it became fashionable for wealthy Roman families to have a Sicilian cook. A Sicilian recipe for minestrone appears in Apicius's *De Re coquinaria* (*Cooking and Dining in Imperial Rome*). *Macco*, a puree of fava beans with wild fennel, also dates back to classical times. It was only natural to make such dishes: all you needed to do was pick what was at hand. Even today, if I arrive at Regaleali and find the refrigerator empty, I go out and pick some wild bitter greens, cook them, and eat them alone like that or with pasta and cheese.

The ingredients of that first recorded minestrone still grow in our gardens: onions, cabbage, zucchini, artichokes, and cardoons. Favas, too, are cultivated; fennel still grows wild. Our herbs are the stuff of myth: mint, oregano, sage, bay, rosemary, and thyme, as well as basil and parsley in summer. They are used singly or together to garnish a dish or flavor a sauce. Other ingredients are often paired as well—olives and capers in *Caponata di Melanzane*, for example, or pine nuts and dried currants, one of the most typical of Sicilian flavor combinations.

When the Arabs arrived around the year 800, they created our national dish. The legend is that when Euphemius landed with his troops, he sent them out to forage for food. They returned with sardines from the sea, wild fennel from the fields, currants from the vines, pine nuts from the trees, and saffron from the flowers. The cooks put them all together and came up with *Pasta con le Sarde*, which remains to this day emblematic of Sicilian cuisine.

The Arabs ruled Sicily for about three hundred years. During that time, they installed their superior agricultural technology, especially their sophisticated methods of irrigation, which vastly improved productivity. They also introduced the cultivation of sugarcane. Sugar replaced honey as a sweetener and as a component of the sweet-and-sour sauces that were, and still are, characteristic of Sicilian cooking. Ever since then, Sicilians have had a sweet tooth. We routinely add sugar to many dishes, especially tomatoes, and we love very sweet pastries and candied fruits.

The Arabs also introduced the cultivation of rice. Nowadays Sicily is too arid to grow rice, but rice has not lost its place in our culinary repertoire. There are even some who whisper that risotto was invented in Sicily. I won't insist on that, though it is true that many of our traditional rice dishes, like *Arancine* and *Ghineffi di Riso*, start with risotto.

Planting citrus, both in gardens and in orchards, was also encouraged by the Arabs. An incredible quantity and variety of citrus are now grown in Sicily. We use the fruit in a thousand different ways, from fresh-squeezed juice to salads to garnishes for fish to desserts and marmalades.

The next conquerors to introduce new crops and thereby change the course of Sicilian culinary history were the Spaniards, who brought the tomato and pepper to Sicily. It took a while before the tomato was accepted as food. For a long time it was regarded as poisonous and was shrouded in superstition; it was used only as an ornamental and later a medicinal plant. Now, of course, it is indispensable, and most Sicilians eat *pasta con la salsa* (pasta with tomato sauce) every day. Many of our pasta dishes can be either *in bianco* or *in rosso*, that is, without or with tomato sauce.

Peppers, too, have become an important ingredient in Sicilian cuisine—big green, red, and yellow sweet peppers in summer and ground dried hot pepper all year round. Doctors say the capsicum pepper is better for your health than black pepper, as long as you don't use too much of it.

The French came before the Spaniards in the Middle Ages but did not add to the Sicilian larder. In the eighteenth century, however, their influence and culture spread through Europe, including Sicily, which felt the influence of their rich cuisine. Cooks were then called Monsieur, which became corrupted to *monzù* in dialect. The cook was the only member of the staff to have such an honorific; everyone else was known by a nickname.

In our household at Regaleali we have the privilege of having a *monzù*, probably the last of the *monzù*, Mario Lo Menzo. He has been with our family since 1954, when he started his apprenticeship with Giovanni Messina. Giovannino, as he was called, had trained in the aristocratic kitchens of Palermo during the Belle Epoque; he reigned as *monzù* from 1914 until his death in 1965 at the age of eighty-eight. In the nine years Mario worked under Giovannino, he learned the old man's secrets—nothing was ever written down—and developed a few of his own. The *cucina baronale* (baronial cuisine) epitomized by Mario calls for a lot of rich ingredients, like butter, cream, and brandy, and fancy French techniques that are not normally used in Sicilian home cooking.

Regaleali has been in my family for almost two hundred years. For much of that time, it was used mainly for the cultivation of wheat, Sicily's major crop for centuries. My grandfather Lucio Tasca inherited the estate at the turn of the century. Under his stewardship, Regaleali became famous as a model farm, winning many prizes for its wheat and animal husbandry. My grandfather also extended the vineyards at Regaleali. The wine was delicious; it was sold from the barrel and bottled only on special occasions. My father, Giuseppe Tasca, took up this activity, expanding the vineyards and wine-making operations. In 1966 he began to bottle the wine commercially.

Like the wine, the food at Regaleali, with few exceptions, is grown and processed on the estate. This is very much in keeping with the Sicilian tradition of self-sufficiency, a tradition made necessary by the island's troubled history and made easy by the extraordinary fertility of the land. Nuts, fruits, and olives grow in abundance; the rich clay soil and long growing season keep the vegetable harvest going for half the year. Sheep provide meat and milk for cheese; chickens and other poultry provide eggs and meat. We are near enough to the sea to enjoy fresh fish on occasion.

One thing those of us who live at Regaleali are proud of is that we like to eat what is raised here. Another is that we all cook. We grew up cooking. My sister Costanza has more success with *minestre* (soups) than anyone, and my mother makes the best *pasta asciutta* (pasta dishes), but we all do the same dishes. Our approach to food is not unique; it is the same with everyone who grew up in the Sicilian countryside and learned to eat off the land.

We Sicilians share a certain philosophy of cooking. We don't make a dish from a recipe; rather we create it from what we have on hand, what is growing on the land at the moment. That way we never cook out of season. We use what is ripe, and we don't keep it for too long. We are not rigid about ingredients—for instance, if there is no basil, we use parsley. We never plan a meal long in advance, unless we have guests. We prefer to cook food and eat our food at once rather than wrap it and store it in the refrigerator for later. Food put on the table straight from the stove tastes so much better than food that is refrigerated and reheated.

Consequently, it has not been easy to write recipes. A few years ago, I began researching old culinary practices that I saw fading away in Sicily, such as making *Estratto di Pomodoro* in the countryside and *pasticcini* and other sweets in the convents. I had also started a cooking school at Regaleali. I knew how to put ingredients and techniques down on paper, but I still had to restrain myself from constantly adapting dishes as I cooked them. When I asked my mother or sister or other people how they made some of their special dishes, they were none too precise. Nor was it easy to get recipes from Mario. To begin with, in the tradition of the *monzù* he carries them all in his head; nothing is written down. And he changes and adapts his recipes as he goes along. For this book, I also wanted to be sure the recipes would work in an American kitchen. When they were tested, things that seemed perfectly obvious to me suddenly turned out to be not clear at all. It took a while to get everything right.

From the beginning, though, I conceived of this book less as a cookbook than as the story of Regaleali. I thought of it as a way to describe the land through the seasons and to portray Sicilian country life. Yet, if years ago someone had told me I would be writing a book, any kind of book, I would have laughed and said, "You're crazy." What happened is this. Ignazio Miceli, our wine distributor, suggested I write about Regaleali to promote the winery. I said no, but the idea caught my imagination, and I began to think about it. I decided to ask my daughter to write the book. She had studied literature and knew how to write, I thought, and perhaps she could make some money as well. But when I read her sample chapter, I could not sleep all night. That was not what I felt toward my land. Fabrizia had been too far away for too long a time. I knew then I had to do it myself—for my family, my friends, the people who work at Regaleali, and, above all, for my grandfather, who taught me to love the earth and the world of nature. I hope I have fulfilled the promise I made to myself early that morning.

Anna Tasca Lanza
Regaleali

Nella Nostra Dispensa

WE ALWAYS HAVE certain products on hand in Sicily, either in the cupboard or refrigerator or, nowadays, in the freezer. Not all of them would normally be kept in a northern European or North American pantry. Certain techniques we use also differ in significant ways from those used elsewhere. Most of these products and techniques are explained as they come up in this book, but I thought it might be a good idea to talk about them all together in one place.

Ingredients

ANCHOVIES

Anchovies are used extensively in Sicilian cooking, both as a flavor accent and as an ingredient in their own right. It is very handy to have a can or a jar of anchovies (flat, not rolled) in the cupboard. Ours are packed in either oil or salt. We put them in salads, in sauces for boiled meat and poached fish, and in certain pasta dishes. They are delicious with mozzarella on toasted bread for a snack.

BOUILLON CUBES

We add bouillon cubes to flavor our sauces, soups, and stews. The ones we use are made from strong broth, usually beef. They have no artificial additives, and they dissolve rapidly. When you use bouillon cubes, you have to add salt and pepper a little at a time, preferably at the end, tasting to be sure not to add too much salt. American friends whom I persuaded to try bouillon cubes have told me that they were pleasantly surprised. Should you choose not to use the cubes, you may substitute a light meat or vegetable stock.

BREAD

Sicilian bread is made with semolina flour, and it is wonderful. From the humblest home to the wealthiest, no meal is complete without bread on the table. Besides eating it fresh, we make *crostini* (toast) to garnish certain dishes and *bruschetta* (grilled bread). The basic topping for *bruschetta* is oil, garlic, and salt. Many other things can be added: anchovy (don't add extra salt), oregano or another herb, tomato with oregano (my favorite), and so on.

Breadcrumbs. When the bread starts to get stale, we put it in a paper bag and hang it in a sheltered place for a few days to dry. Then we crush it and sift it. The most common use for breadcrumbs is in stuffings for fish, meat, and vegetables. We also use breadcrumbs as a garnish for certain pasta-and-fish dishes.

CAPERS

The best Sicilian capers come from the island of Pantelleria, where they grow wild. They are very large. We get them layered in sea salt or pickled in vinegar brine. In the United States, the wild capers that are exported from Greece are most similar to Sicilian capers. You can rinse capers or not, as you like, before adding them to a dish; use them sparingly.

CHEESE

We make our own sheep's milk cheeses at Regaleali: ricotta, *tuma* (curd cheese), *primo sale* (young pecorino), and aged pecorino. It is not easy to find such cheeses in the United States. You can substitute fresh mozzarella or a mild goat cheese for the *tuma* and Parmigiano-Reggiano for grated pecorino, but the ricotta presents a real problem. Although you can sometimes find good ricotta in Italian neighborhoods and through such top-quality purveyors as Paula Lambert's Mozzarella Factory in Dallas, Texas, for example, the American cow's milk ricotta simply does not have the same rich flavor as our sheep's milk ricotta. If your ricotta tastes bland or flat, add some crumbled ricotta salata (for sweet dishes) or mild goat cheese (for savory dishes): a half pound of ricotta salata or goat cheese to a pound of ricotta is about right. Our ricotta also has a different consistency from commercially made cow's milk ricotta; it is not so smooth and it can be drained overnight and sliced the next day. Because of this difference, you may want to substitute slices of ricotta salata in some of the recipes. Besides our own cheeses we buy caciocavallo and melting cheeses like Fontina.

CORNSTARCH

Cornstarch (or wheat starch) rather than flour is used for sweets, because it gives a much lighter effect.

CURRANTS

Dried currants are actually dried tiny grapes. They used to grow in profusion in Sicily, and they are still plentiful and inexpensive. It is traditional to pair them with pine nuts in fillings; we call the combination *passoli e pinoli*. I like to sprinkle the two on my *Insalata di Spinaci alla Siciliana*. Store currants in a jar, with or without pine nuts. If the ones you get seem very dry and hard, soak them in warm water for a few minutes before using.

FLOUR

Wheat remains the grain of choice in Sicily. We use hard-wheat semolina flour for bread and what in Europe is called 00 flour for all other purposes, from sauce thickening to cake and pastry baking. Except for the bread, all of the recipes calling for flour have been tested with unbleached all-purpose flour.

GARLIC

Garlic is not as vital a seasoning in Sicilian cooking as it is in northern Italian and French cuisine. When fresh garlic is in season and I can go out in the garden and pick it (I always plant some to keep the aphids away from my roses), I use that. Like all fresh vegetables, it gives the dish a milder flavor. When the garlic can no longer stay in the earth, we pick it all, braid it, and hang it to dry.

GELATIN

In Europe, gelatin is usually processed in sheets, but the recipes in this book were tested with the granular gelatin that is packaged in envelopes.

HERBS

We use herbs by the handful when we cook, and we are lucky to have most herbs with us all year long, except basil and parsley. What follows is a brief description of the herbs most commonly used in Sicilian cooking and at Regaleali.

Basil. Sicilian basil is very pungent, and we use it fresh all summer long. When the plants begin to go to seed, we pick the leaves and freeze them to tide us over the winter. Use basil leaves whole or shred them at the last minute before adding them to a dish.

Bay. Since bay trees, which are evergreen, grow at Regaleali, we have fresh bay all year-round. It has a much more pleasant aroma than the dried. The dried Turkish bay leaves I have smelled in the United States are stronger than ours, so I have been cautious about amounts. If a recipe calls for fresh bay leaves and you don't have any, soak some dried ones until they soften.

Mint. Mint gives a refreshing twist to many fish, meat, and vegetable dishes. I like to add a few leaves to a salad. It's a must in sweet-and-sour sauces. We always use it fresh.

Oregano. All the oregano we use is dried; it has a much stronger flavor than the fresh. To dry your own, cut it when it is in full bloom (first thing in the morning for maximum flavor) and hang it in a cool place. When it is completely dry, crush it by rubbing it between the palms of your hands over a piece of newspaper so that it doesn't fly all over the place. Sift it and store it in a jar. It will keep for about two years. You can also dry the oregano in a low (150°F.) oven.

Parsley. Our parsley is the flat-leaf kind, which is sometimes called Italian parsley; it has a much deeper flavor than the curly, so-called French parsley. My father could not live without it. Mario puts it on just about everything—pasta, potatoes, vegetables prepared *a spezzatino* (braised), fish, and so on. We freeze huge quantities of chopped parsley in summer to be sure we always have it when we need it.

OVERLEAF: *Capers, hot peppers, garlic, oregano, and bay lend Sicilian food their savor.*

Rosemary. Bushes of rosemary grow everywhere at Regaleali. It was planted for the bees, but we enjoy it too. Its penetrating aroma is perfect with lamb and poultry.

Sage. Though strongly scented, sage is mostly used in delicate dishes, usually in combination with butter and parmesan. It is also a good addition to a mixed-herb garnish.

Thyme. Thyme adds a special touch when cooked with meat or poultry. I like to sprinkle leaves of it on *Insalata di Finocchio e Cedro.*

Wild Fennel. Wild fennel grows everywhere in Sicily; it comes out with the fall rains and lasts until May or June. We pick it as we need it; at the end of the season, we gather as much as we can and freeze it. If you have the good luck to get some wild fennel from a gardener or forager, use some of it fresh, then blanch and freeze the rest of the stalks and fronds. Wild fennel seeds are used as a flavoring, particularly for sausage.

HONEY

We have our own honey at Regaleali. The hives are behind the chapel, and Pinuzzo Ognibene, the beekeeper, is very proud of the honey he gets from them. It tastes like wildflowers or fruit blossoms, rosemary or eucalyptus, depending on what is in bloom when you remove the honey. The honey is refined, and we use it mainly on bread and butter at breakfast, on ricotta, and for some desserts, such as *Pignoccata.* Sometimes I put a drop in salad dressing.

LEGUMES AND DRIED BEANS

We do not have so many dishes using legumes and dried beans as they do in northern Europe, except in winter. Then a steaming bowl of lentil or bean soup is very welcome indeed. We use several kinds of dried beans, mostly *borlotti,* which are similar to the cranberry beans of North America. We also dry peas and favas and make soup with them in winter.

Chick-peas. Chick-peas are dried and ground into flour, which is used for *Panelle.* It is traditional to serve chick-peas on the feast of Santa Lucia. There is a soup made with chick-peas. It takes hours to cook and days to digest. Not everyone likes it.

LEMONS

Sicily is the land of the lemon, a lemon that is very perfumed and not too sour. Both the peel and the juice are used in cooking. Sicilians even like to eat the flesh of the lemon, and sometimes we put it in tomato salad. Grated lemon peel is traditionally used to flavor cakes and pastry. The juice goes into sauces, liaisons, salad dressings, and many other dishes. When lemons are in season in winter, we freeze as much juice as we can for lemonade and cold tea in the summer.

OILS AND FATS

We use mostly olive oil but also other oils and fats, suiting them to the dishes we are cooking. Sometimes we differ among ourselves as to which one is better with which dish.

Butter. We make our own butter, and we use a lot of it. Generally speaking, though, butter is not much used in the Sicilian kitchen. For most purposes olive oil, a traditional product of the land that does not require refrigeration, is preferred. Butter is always used in pastry dough and in *brasciamella* (béchamel). Mario has a heavy hand with butter, using spoons by the dozen; I have a lighter touch. We always use unsalted butter.

Lard. In the past, a *monzù* would have used only *sugna* (lard) for frying—it was believed to make fried foods crisper—and we still use it to fry traditional foods like *sfince.* I prefer vegetable oil, and that is what I recommend for these recipes. We also use lard sometimes for pastry if we want a crisper crust.

Margarine. It shocks some people to see that we use margarine, not as a spread, of course, but in cooking. I find that combining margarine with butter in certain preparations gives better results than butter alone.

Olive Oil. We grow our own olives and have them pressed for oil. Not surprisingly, we use a lot of it in cooking: to sauté onions and garlic as a base for many dishes, to dress salads, and to drizzle over soup. All the olive oil we use is extra virgin.

Vegetable Oil. For deep-fat frying, we use vegetable oil, which imparts a light flavor.

OLIVES

Always on hand are black and green olives to serve as a snack or a garnish. We also cook with them. Our black olives are oil cured; the green ones preserved in brine. It may be difficult to find good-quality oil-cured black olives in the United States. Keep trying and tasting different ones imported from different countries until you find some that taste right. You'll probably have better luck with green olives.

ONIONS

Onions are very important in Sicilian cooking. Chopped onions are sautéed in olive oil to make a base for sauces and stuffings; thinly sliced raw onions are put into salads; thicker wedges are tucked into brochettes or added to meat that is to be roasted. Most of the time we use large red sweet onions, but when they are not available, we substitute yellow onions. We also use shallots and small onions from time to time.

PASTA

The pasta we eat in Sicily is dried hard-wheat pasta that we buy in a box. We use mostly spaghetti, capellini, and perciatelli (also called bucatino). Anelletti, a chewy ring-shaped pasta, is traditionally served with a thick meat *ragù* sauce.

Pasta Water. Sometimes a bit of the water in which the pasta was cooked is added to a sauce to bring it to the desired consistency. The easiest way to do this is to remove a ladleful or two of water from the pot shortly before draining the pasta and thin the sauce. Drain the pasta when it is ready and mix it with the sauce as usual.

PINE NUTS

As the name suggests, pine nuts come from a pine tree; the kernels hide in the cones. Pine nuts are used extensively in Sicilian cooking—in fillings (usually in combination with currants), in pesto, and in sweets. Store pine nuts in a jar in the refrigerator.

PORK PRODUCTS

At Regaleali we do not cook with cured-pork products as much as some others do. We use mostly *prosciutto cotto* (boiled ham) and pancetta, or unsmoked bacon, which I hear is more widely available in the United States than it used to be. Blanched smoked bacon is an acceptable substitute. We use fennel-flavored pork sausage in *ragù*, and we grill it. This sausage is similar to what is called sweet Italian sausage in the United States. There is always some at hand when summer has gone by.

RICE

Rice was grown in Sicily many years ago, and it remains an ingredient in many traditional dishes. We use Arborio rice from northern Italy; this is what you should use in these recipes.

SALT

There are vast salt flats around Trapani in western Sicily, where salt is produced by evaporation. I think sea salt is the best for cooking. If you use another kind, you have to add twice as much to get the same result, but most of the recipes in this book call for salt "to taste" so you can adjust it to please your own palate.

SPICES AND OTHER SEASONINGS

Sicilian food is well seasoned, both in the kitchen and at the table. In addition to salt, we use the following seasonings.

Hot Pepper. Peperoncino in polvere (ground hot pepper) is used in the kitchen, and there is always a shaker of it on the table. The best is what you make yourself. Put some whole hot peppers in a very low (150°F.) oven for about an hour to dry, then crush them to a fine powder in a spice mill. Hot paprika is a good substitute, better than cayenne, which has a harsher taste. We also make *olio al peperoncino* (hot pepper–flavored oil). We put a few drops in soup, especially bean and lentil soups. To make it, fill a jar with fresh whole hot peppers and add oil to cover. Let it stand for a couple of months before using. The oil becomes very hot, so add just a drop or two at a time. In general, be careful when seasoning with hot pepper—if you add too much, you'll end up tasting nothing.

Pepper. We use black pepper, freshly ground in a pepper mill. When pepper is called for in a recipe, that is the kind to use.

Saffron. Saffron is an ancient flavoring of Sicilian food. It grows wild in the Madonie Mountains in central Sicily, but it is very tedious to pick. Saffron is cultivated in Abruzzi on the mainland and in Spain. We now grow something called false saffron at Regaleali. It is a sort of thistle, much easier to gather, but not as tasty as the real thing. We use saffron in fish soup and *spezzatino* and some pasta dishes, most famously *Pasta con le Sarde.* Saffron is also often used to add color and flavor to rice.

SUGAR

The Arabs introduced sugar to Sicily in the ninth century, and we have cooked with it ever since. Some visitors find our pastries cloyingly sweet and are surprised to learn that we put sugar in our tomato sauce. We are also very fond of sweet-and-sour sauces.

TOMATOES

No Sicilian kitchen would be without tomatoes, fresh all summer long and preserved the rest of the year. We grow plum tomatoes (Roma and San Marzano) for preserving in *salse* (sauces) and *Estratto di Pomodoro.* Where a recipe calls for *estratto,* you can substitute sun-dried tomato paste, using about three times as much paste. If you can't find sun-dried tomato paste, use regular tomato paste. We also grow salad and beefsteak tomatoes and cherry tomatoes to eat off the vine.

TUNA (CANNED)

We always have some canned tuna on hand to make one pasta sauce or another or to fill in when someone doesn't like what is on the table. Fortunately we are able to get excellent albacore tuna packed in olive oil. If you can't find that, substitute solid white tuna packed in oil. In either case, rinse off the oil first, since you will be using a better-quality oil in the dish.

VINEGAR

Vinegar, mostly red wine vinegar, has many uses in the Sicilian kitchen. We combine it with olive oil for salad dressing and with sugar for sweet-and-sour sauces. We steep fish in vinegar before frying. I preserve such vegetables as eggplant and mushrooms in white wine vinegar, which I make myself. At Regaleali, all the vinegar comes from our own wine; any good vinegar with a nice flavor will be fine in these recipes.

WINE

Since Mario is heir to the *monzù* tradition, which favors wine and spirits in cooking, we have some special dishes in which the wine goes in by the bottleful. When you cook with wine, remember that there is no such thing as "cooking wine." Anything you put in the pot should be good enough to pour in a glass.

Cooking Techniques

For the most part, Sicilian cooking techniques are the same as those of northern Europe or North America. But there are some for which our style seems to be unique and that made a difference when the recipes were tested in an American kitchen. They seem to me of primary importance. That is why I mention them.

MAKING BÉCHAMEL

When we make béchamel, which is called *brasciamella* in Sicily and *besciamella* in mainland Italy, we melt the butter in a saucepan, remove it from the heat, and whisk in the flour. Then we put the saucepan back on the stove and add the milk gradually, without cooking the flour first. We use the milk cold.

SAUTÉING

We don't heat the oil before sautéing; we put everything in the skillet at once, cold, then turn on the heat. The garlic and onions are cooked until limp and slightly golden. If you are standing in front of the stove, you can do this over high heat, shaking the pan often. Or you can do it over low heat, shaking the pan from time to time. We brown meat this way, too, starting with cold ingredients in a cold pan.

COOKING PASTA

For us Sicilians, cooking and eating pasta are almost a religious rite. We like our pasta, particularly spaghetti and capellini, more al dente than people elsewhere do. Exactly how done the spaghetti should be is always a matter of debate—if there are four Sicilians sitting at the table, there will be four opinions, but all will agree that getting it to the desired point of doneness requires very close attention. Thicker kinds of pasta, like perciatelli and rigatoni, are more forgiving than the thin. They are cooked longer than spaghetti—until tender—and they can also stand for a minute or two. These are a better choice than spaghetti if you can't get the pasta from the pot to the table in seconds for one reason or another. Here is how to cook spaghetti the Sicilian way.

First, have everything ready—a big pot with a lid, a long fork next to the stove, a colander in the sink, and next to the sink a serving dish with a little butter or oil in it. Fill the pot with water, add salt (one or two tablespoons to five quarts of water for one pound of spaghetti), cover, and bring to a rolling boil. Add the spaghetti—without breaking the strands—while holding the fork in your other hand. Stir with the fork to separate the strands immediately. Cover the pot and bring it back to a boil as quickly as possible. This is one of the stages during which the spaghetti can go soft if you do not take care.

Remove the lid when the water comes back to a boil, and adjust the heat so the water continues to bubble hard but does not boil over. From this point on, do not leave the stove. Do not even reach over to answer the telephone. Stand right there in front of the pot. After five minutes, start tasting for salt and doneness. Spaghetti usually takes about ten minutes to be done, but sometimes a new brand plays dirty tricks on you and is ready before you expect.

A moment before the spaghetti has reached the ideal point—when it is al dente, or still firm to the bite—remove the pot from the heat and drain the spaghetti in the colander you put in the sink before starting. Do not bother to turn off the heat as this is another delicate moment when the spaghetti can get soggy if left floating in the hot water. Shake the colander once or twice, then transfer the spaghetti to the serving dish and dress it immediately with some of the sauce. Never leave the spaghetti standing in the colander, not even for a minute. It will get soggy and stick together. Put the rest of the sauce on top of the spaghetti and bring the dish to the table right away. Everyone will be sitting there waiting to be served. When Sicilians eat spaghetti, conversation ceases. They start talking again only when they have finished eating the sacred dish.

La Primavera

‖ S P R I N G ‖

Spring comes early to Sicily.

In February, while the rest of Europe is cold and dark,

the twisted almond trees spread their pale pink-and-white mantle over

the emerald hills. After a pause, the fruit trees bloom in swift

succession—sour cherry (which grows wild alongside the bamboo

in the streambeds), apricot, plum, and cherry, one

after the other, casting a perfumed veil across the ravines and valleys.

Even though I know the moment of nature's awakening

will come as it does every year, the sheer beauty of it

takes my breath away.

THE FIELDS ARE TRANSFORMED into vast patches of color, mostly purple from the cloverlike flower of *sulla* (French honeysuckle) and green, every shade from the palest to the most intense. Wildflowers bloom at the edge of the road: red poppies, yellow broom, chamomile, wood sorrel, and tiny wild orchids. The orchids have become very rare, but you can still find some at Regaleali. Wild roses grow everywhere, and I take them to make very pretty decorations for the big dining table when we have guests. Queen Anne's lace and the giant wild fennel are rampant too, and I often make a centerpiece with their white and yellow flowers.

The giant fennel is inedible, but we use a smaller kind of wild fennel in the kitchen to flavor sauces and soups, like *Minestra delle Ultime Fave.* Wild fennel is an essential flavoring of Sicilian cooking. We use a lot when it is in season, and we always freeze some.

While the wild fennel is still fresh, Mario Lo Menzo, our *monzù* chef, is sure to make the famous Sicilian dish *Pasta con le Sarde.* All the classic elements are in it: fennel from the earth, fish from the sea, pine nuts from the trees, dried currants from the vine, saffron from flowers, and that most Sicilian of ingredients, pasta. At heart, though, it is the marriage of wild fennel and ultrafresh sardines that makes this dish so extraordinary.

Wild fennel is very difficult to find in the United States. Some Sicilian-Americans plant it in their gardens for a taste of home. It grows in California, and I have heard that growers there are trying to cultivate wild fennel for sale. If you are lucky enough to find it, use some fresh, then blanch and freeze the rest. As for the sardines, the ones I have seen, on both coasts of North America, have all been out of the water too long for this dish. But for that enchanted day when you find truly fresh sardines and truly wild fennel, I'll give you the recipe.

PASTA CON LE SARDE *Pasta with Sardines and Wild Fennel*

2 pounds fresh wild fennel

3 pounds whole fresh sardines, scaled, cleaned, boned, heads, tails, and top fins removed
(about 1 1/2 pounds after preparation)

Semolina flour, for coating

1 1/4 cups olive oil

2 medium onions, minced

1 cup Salsa di Pomodoro Passata (page 114)

3 tablespoons pine nuts

3 tablespoons dried currants

6 anchovy fillets

1 teaspoon grated nutmeg

Salt

Black pepper

8 saffron threads or 1/2 teaspoon powdered saffron

1 1/2 pounds perciatelli

Boil the fennel in salted water for about 20 minutes, or until tender. Drain, reserving 1 cup of the cooking water, and chop fine. Set the fennel aside.

Reserve 4 or 5 sardines for garnish. Coat these in semolina flour and fry in 1/4 cup of the olive oil. Drain on paper towels and set them aside.

Sauté the onions in the remaining olive oil for 6 to 8 minutes, or until just golden. Add the fennel, salsa, pine nuts, currants, anchovies, nutmeg, and salt and pepper to taste. Bring to a boil, reduce the heat, and cook for 15 to 20 minutes, stirring frequently. Add the remaining sardines and cook for about 15 minutes, stirring from time to time, or until the sardines break up. If the sauce becomes too thick, add the reserved fennel water.

Dissolve the saffron in 2 to 3 tablespoons warm water and set aside. Cook the perciatelli in boiling salted water until tender. Drain the pasta, return it to the cooking pot, and toss it with the saffron water. Let it stand for about 2 minutes to allow the saffron to color and season the pasta.

Turn the perciatelli into a serving bowl, add half of the sauce, and mix thoroughly. Cover with the remaining sauce and garnish with the fried sardines. Let stand for about 5 minutes to allow the flavors to develop. This will easily serve 8 to 10 as a first course. It is very rich.

‖ *Fava Beans* ‖

The very first fava beans appear on the table on March 19, the feast of San Giuseppe. These young beans are very tender, crisp, and juicy, and we eat them raw, sometimes with pecorino cheese. More often, though, we serve them with the fresh fruit in the fruit basket that is placed on the table at the end of every meal.

The season for favas lasts quite a long time—through May—which is probably why we have so many ways of preparing them. The very first beans to mature, *le prime fave*, we sauté *a spezzatino* with finely chopped onion and parsley. This way of preparing vegetables also works well with artichokes, zucchini, peas, and potatoes. You start by frying onion (and sometimes garlic) in olive oil, then adding the vegetable and a little liquid, usually wine and water. With many vegetables you can add a little more liquid to make a sauce for pasta or you can add a lot more liquid and a beef bouillon cube to make a soup.

When the beans are tender, crisp, and juicy, we serve them with spaghetti in *Pasta con le Favuzze Fresche*. The favas have a surprisingly delicate flavor and muted gray-green color.

PASTA CON LE FAVUZZE FRESCHE *Pasta with Fresh Fava Beans*

1 1/2 cups chopped onion
1 garlic clove, finely chopped
1/2 cup olive oil
1 to 1 1/2 cups shelled fava beans (1 to 1 1/2 pounds in the pod)
1/2 cup chopped parsley
1 cup water
Salt
1 pound spaghetti

Sauté the onion and garlic in the olive oil in a medium saucepan until soft, about 5 minutes. Add the fava beans, half the parsley, and the water. Cover and cook until tender, about 10 minutes for fresh young fava beans. Add salt to taste.

Cook the spaghetti in boiling salted water until al dente. Drain. Pour half the sauce into a large serving bowl, add the pasta, and toss. Put the remaining sauce on top and sprinkle with the remaining parsley. Serve the pasta immediately. This will serve 4 as a first course.

We also combine the early favas with peas and artichokes in *Frittella*. There are two versions of this spring medley. One is served warm; the other is marinated in a sweet-and-sour sauce and is eaten cold.

FRITTELLA *Fresh Vegetable Medley*

³/₄ pound small artichokes

2 medium onions, minced

¹/₃ cup olive oil

1 cup shelled fava beans (about 1 pound in the pod)

1 cup fresh or frozen peas

1¹/₂ cups water

Salt

Black pepper

Salsa Agrodolce (optional)

¹/₂ cup white wine vinegar

1 tablespoon sugar

8 to 10 mint leaves, plus additional for garnish

Prepare the artichokes as described on page 44. Set aside in lemon water.

Sauté the onions in the olive oil for 2 to 3 minutes, until just golden. Add the fava beans and cook for 5 minutes. Drain the artichokes, add them, and cook for another 5 minutes. Add the peas and 1 cup of the water and cook for up to 15 minutes more for fresh and about 5 minutes more for frozen. Season to taste with salt and pepper. Cover and cook, stirring from time to time, until all the vegetables are tender, about 15 minutes. Add additional water as needed. Serve warm if desired.

To serve cold, make a Salsa Agrodolce by adding the vinegar, sugar, and mint leaves to the pan after the vegetables have cooked for 10 minutes. Boil, stirring occasionally, until the sugar dissolves, about 5 minutes. Refrigerate the vegetables and serve cold, garnished with mint leaves.

This will serve 4 as a first course.

As time goes on, the skin of the fava grows tough, and it becomes necessary to peel the beans. At this stage, they have a stronger taste and brighter color than before. They can be blanched and sautéed in butter as a side dish with meat. Or they can be used for a pasta dish that we call *Pasta con le Fave Spicchiate* (Pasta with Split Fava Beans) because the peeled beans fall apart into segments. In this dish, everything is stronger. The beans are braised with pancetta, tomatoes, and white wine—which would overwhelm *le prime fave*— and served with perciatelli and grated pecorino.

When the favas get even bigger, we make *fave bollite* (boiled favas) and serve the beans with a mixture of oil, vinegar, and salt for dipping. The only way to eat these favas is to pick one up with your fingers, dip it, put it in your mouth, and suck the bean out of the

Pasta con le Sarde (page 35) is made with the first wild fennel of the season and sardines fresh from the sea. Wild roses grow near the entry of Case Grandi, and almond blossoms perfume the spring air.

skin, making awful noises. My daughter, Fabrizia, who now lives in Verona, says it is one of the dishes from home she misses most.

Finally, we make a special fava bean soup, *Minestra delle Ultime Fave*. When people turn up at Case Vecchie, the old farm buildings where I have an apartment, at the end of the fava season in May, what I often do is give them each a basket and take them out to the garden to pick the last favas from the withered plants. On the way home, we pick some wild fennel. Then I hand each person a knife, and we all sit down and peel the favas, removing both the pod and the hard skin of the bean. When the favas are ready, we put the soup on to cook and bid the season *addio*.

MINESTRA DELLE ULTIME FAVE *Fava Bean Soup*

1 medium onion, sliced
2 cups shelled and peeled end-of-season fava beans (about 2 pounds in the pod)
1 chicken or beef bouillon cube
6 cups water
¹/₂ cup coarsely chopped wild fennel
Salt
Black pepper
Olive oil, for garnish
Croutons, for garnish

Combine the onion, favas, bouillon cube, and water in a medium saucepan. Bring the mixture to a boil, reduce the heat, and simmer until the beans start to break apart, at least 20 minutes. Add the fennel and season to taste with salt and pepper. Drizzle with olive oil and garnish with croutons. This is enough for 4.

Garden Peas

Peas ripen at the same time as fava beans, but their season in Sicily is exceedingly brief. You must catch them when they are ready, for a day or two later they are like little bullets. So we pick them all in the course of a week, eat what we can, and freeze the rest. A nice way to prepare fresh peas is *Piselli a Spezzatino con Prosciutto.* These peas with ham can be used to fill a *Sformato di Spinaci.*

PISELLI A SPEZZATINO CON PROSCIUTTO *Braised Peas with Ham*

1 small red onion, minced
3 tablespoons olive oil
2 cups fresh or frozen peas
2 tablespoons white wine
1 1/2 cups water
1/4 cup chopped boiled ham
Salt
Black pepper

Sauté the onion in the olive oil until it's soft, about 5 minutes. Stir in the peas, the wine, and the water. Cover and cook until the peas are tender, 20 to 30 minutes for fresh, less for frozen. Stir in the ham. Season to taste with salt and pepper. This serves 4 to 6 as a side dish.

Once the peas are hard, the only thing you can do with them is make *Purè di Piselli.* This is a thick soup, like a French potage, with an egg-yolk liaison added at the end to keep it from separating.

Sicilians make soup with bouillon cubes; we find they have no equal when it comes to bringing out flavors. If you prefer, you can substitute a light meat or vegetable stock, but the soup will not be as good as ours, nor will it be truly Sicilian.

PURÈ DI PISELLI *Pea Soup*

2 cups whole sugar snap peas, trimmed, or 2 cups frozen peas

1 beef bouillon cube

Salt

Black pepper

1 egg yolk

3 to 3½ tablespoons milk

2 tablespoons butter, softened

3 tablespoons grated parmesan

½ cup cooked rice (optional)

Croutons, for garnish (optional)

Grated parmesan, for garnish

Simmer the peas in water to cover, uncovered, until thoroughly softened, 20 to 30 minutes (less with frozen peas). Puree, using a food mill or food processor. (If you use a food processor, strain the puree.) Return the puree to the saucepan and add enough water to make a thick soup. Add the bouillon cube and cook until it dissolves. Add salt and pepper to taste.

Put the egg yolk, milk, butter, and parmesan in the bottom of a soup tureen and whisk to blend. Whisk about ½ cup of the soup into the egg mixture, then gradually stir in the rest. Taste and adjust the seasonings. Stir in the rice, if using, or garnish with croutons. Sprinkle the soup with more parmesan and serve warm. Do not reheat. This serves 4 to 6 as a first course.

While both the peas and fava beans are young and tender, we often combine them in a soup, *Minestra di Fave e Piselli.* Unlike the *Purè di Piselli,* it is a clear soup, and we add spaghetti, broken into one-inch pieces, either cooked in the soup or separately.

Since all of our vegetable soups are made the same way, you can use this recipe as a model and substitute other vegetables—escarole or broccoli or cauliflower or just about anything you can think of—for the peas and favas and get good results.

MINESTRA DI FAVE E PISELLI *Fava Bean and Garden Pea Soup*

1 medium onion, finely chopped

3 tablespoons olive oil

1 cup shelled fava beans (about 1 pound in the pod), peeled if tough

1 cup fresh or frozen peas

1 beef bouillon cube

2 tablespoons Salsa di Pomodoro Passata (page 114) or 1 medium tomato, peeled, seeded,
  and chopped (optional)

6 to 7 cups water

1 cup broken-up spaghetti or spaghettini, preferably cooked and drained

Salt

Black pepper

Olive oil, for garnish

Grated parmesan, for garnish

Sauté the onion in the oil in a medium saucepan until just golden, 2 to 3 minutes.
Add the favas and peas, stirring to coat. Add the bouillon cube, salsa, if you like, and
1 cup of the water. Bring to a boil, then reduce the heat and simmer gently until the
vegetables are nearly tender, about 25 minutes. Add 5 cups more water, bring the
soup back to a boil, add the spaghetti, and heat until warm. If you use uncooked
pasta, add the remaining cup of water, bring the soup to a boil, and cook until the
spaghetti is al dente. Season to taste with salt and pepper. Drizzle some olive oil
on top, sprinkle with grated cheese, and serve. This soup is enough for 4 to 6 as a
first course.

Artichokes

Artichokes begin to ripen in late February or early March, around the same time as the
first favas and peas, but in the shops those early artichokes are so expensive few people
buy them. Fortunately, the price comes down fast, and we have fresh artichokes all the
way through May.

The Sicilian artichoke is about four inches long and two inches thick in the middle,
with thorn-tipped violet-and-green "leaves." The vendors offer them for sale with about
two feet of stem and the silvery-green leaves of the plants still attached. They are a beautiful sight, piled up in the stalls and barrows of the market.

While the artichokes are still very tender, we eat them raw in salad, later in a hundred different ways—whole or cut up, hot or cold, boiled, braised, or roasted. I don't know if you can find artichokes tender enough to eat raw, but my artichoke salad, *Insalata di Carciofi*, is so good it is definitely worth a try. It has a very unusual flavor.

CLEANING ARTICHOKES

The initial preparation of artichokes is the same for all our artichoke dishes, except *Carciofi alla Brace*. It may seem time-consuming at first, but once you get the knack of it, it goes fast. You need to use lemons when you prepare artichokes, both to keep them from darkening and to prevent them from staining your hands.

Start by squeezing a couple of lemons into a large bowl. Add about two cups of water and drop in the lemon halves. Cut another lemon in half and keep it handy. Bend back and break off all the tough outer leaves of the artichoke. Cut off the remaining leaves about an inch and a half from the tip. Rub the artichoke with lemon or place it in a half lemon and turn, as if reaming the lemon. Cut the artichoke in half and drop one half into the lemon water while you remove the choke from the other half, using the tip of a sharp knife. Rub the half artichoke all over with lemon and drop it into the lemon water. Clean the choke from the other half. Continue until all the artichokes you need are done. Remember to rub your hands with lemon from time to time to prevent staining.

INSALATA DI CARCIOFI *Raw Artichoke Salad*

4 small artichokes
3 tablespoons red wine vinegar
1/2 cup olive oil
1/4 cup chopped parsley
Salt

Prepare the artichokes as described above. Slice the artichoke halves lengthwise into 1/4-inch slices and return to the lemon water. Combine the vinegar, oil, parsley, and salt to taste in the bottom of a salad bowl. Drain the artichokes well, add them to the dressing, and toss to combine. Taste and adjust the seasoning. If the taste of the lemon is too strong, add more salt to the salad to correct the balance. This salad serves 2.

One of my favorite artichoke dishes is *Caponata di Carciofi*, an antipasto in which the artichokes are steeped in a sauce made with olives and celery. You start by preparing *Carciofi a Spezzatino*—that is to say, by braising the artichokes. Like the *Frittella*, the *Caponata* has a typically Sicilian sweet-and-sour flavor.

CARCIOFI A SPEZZATINO *Braised Artichokes*

12 small artichokes
1 medium onion, finely chopped
2 garlic cloves, minced
1/3 cup olive oil
1/4 cup white wine
1/3 cup water
1/2 chicken bouillon cube
2 teaspoons chopped parsley
Salt
Black pepper

Prepare the artichokes as described on page 44. Slice the artichokes in 1/2-inch wedges and return them to the lemon water until you're ready for them.

Sauté the onion and garlic in the olive oil in a medium sauté pan for 2 to 3 minutes, until just golden. Drain the artichokes and add them to the pan. Stir in the wine, water, bouillon cube, and parsley. Cover and simmer for 15 minutes. Season to taste with salt and pepper. You can serve these warm or at room temperature. As a side dish, it's enough for 4.

CAPONATA DI CARCIOFI *Artichoke Caponata*

1 cup Salsa di Pomodoro Passata (page 114)
1/2 cup green olives, pitted
1 tablespoon capers, rinsed
1 stalk celery, minced
1/2 cup red wine vinegar
1 tablespoon sugar
Carciofi a Spezzatino (above), slightly undercooked
Salt
Black pepper

Combine the salsa, olives, capers, and celery in a medium saucepan and simmer for 15 minutes, or until thickened. Raise the heat, add the vinegar and sugar, and boil for about 2 minutes. Remove from the heat, add the spezzatino, and gently combine. Let cool, then add salt and pepper to taste. Serve this as an appetizer or side dish at room temperature; it makes about 3 cups or enough to serve 6.

Artichokes are stuffed with garlic and dried oregano and doused with olive oil, then set directly in the coals. They are so delicious you could eat a dozen of them (page 48). Oregano grows everywhere, even among the prickly pears in front of Case Vecchie. Wild red poppies and purple onion blossoms brighten the fields and gardens.

There is another wonderful artichoke dish that we unfortunately do not have often enough—*Carciofi alla Brace* (Artichokes on the Coals). For this you trim away the thorns and tips of the leaves, then, holding an artichoke in your hand, spread the leaves apart with your thumbs and push a mixture of garlic, salt, pepper, and dried oregano down between the leaves. Just before cooking, pour olive oil into the center. After you have finished with the meat or whatever you are cooking on the grill, and the coals have burned down, set the artichokes directly in the cinders and give them a quarter turn from time to time so that they cook evenly. The artichokes are ready when they are completely charred. To eat them, discard the outer leaves and bite off the flesh from the bottom of the remaining leaves. These artichokes are so delicious you could eat a dozen of them, if only they did not come, as they always do, at the end of a big meal.

A more formal way to prepare artichokes is gratinéed. First the completely trimmed artichokes have to be cooked in a *blanc* of flour, lemon juice, and water so they stay pale. *Carciofi Gratinati* can be used to fill and garnish *Sformato di Spinaci,* but they are quite delicious on their own as a first dish.

CARCIOFI GRATINATI *Artichoke Gratin*

16 small artichokes
1 cup flour
6 cups water
6 tablespoons freshly squeezed lemon juice
Salt
2 tablespoons butter
2 tablespoons grated parmesan

Prepare the artichokes as described on page 44. Pour about 3 cups of the water into a medium saucepan and whisk in the flour. Bring to a boil, whisking from time to time, to make sure the liquid is without lumps. Whisk in the remaining water, 4 tablespoons of the lemon juice, and salt to taste. This makes the blanc for cooking the artichokes.

Put the artichoke halves in the saucepan and add additional water to cover, if necessary. Bring to a boil, reduce the heat, and simmer until tender, about 15 minutes. Drain the artichokes, cover, and set aside.

Shortly before serving, preheat the oven to 375° F. Butter an 8×10-inch baking dish.

Arrange the artichoke halves, cut side down, in the baking dish, dot with butter, and sprinkle with the remaining lemon juice and the parmesan. Bake until the cheese

begins to melt, 10 to 15 minutes. Do not brown. This makes about 3 cups of gratinati, which you can use to garnish and fill a Sformato di Spinaci. It will also serve 6 as
a side dish.

Spinach and Swiss Chard

In Palermo, you can find spinach and *giri* (chard) in the shops throughout the year, but I
find that what I grow myself, regardless of season, tastes better, especially when freshly
picked and steamed. We have two kinds of chard, the familiar one, with a big leaf and a
large white rib down the center, and a smaller and leafier one, with almost no rib at all.
Since there is new growth after you cut off the leaves, you can have it all year round. We
use it like spinach. A puree of this chard, made with milk, butter, and parmesan and
served with poached eggs, is absolutely delicious. Mario makes a spinach ring and fills it
with artichokes or peas and ham for special occasions. He calls it a flan, in the French
style, and his recipe is very rich. I prefer to use this simpler version. On informal occasions, you can pack the *Sformato di Spinaci* in a loaf pan and serve it with melted Fontina
cheese. The *sformato* is also good made with Swiss chard or wild greens or a mixture of
the two. Like *Carciofi Gratinati, Piselli a Spezzatino con Prosciutto* can be used to fill the ring.

OVERLEAF: *The Sformato di Spinaci (page 52) is garnished with Carciofi Gratinati and dressed with a rich
sauce from Agglassato.*

SFORMATO DI SPINACI *Spinach Mold*

9 pounds fresh spinach, stemmed
1¾ cups grated parmesan
Salt
Black pepper
5 eggs
3 tablespoons butter
Piselli a Spezzatino con Prosciutto (page 41, optional)
Carciofi Gratinati (page 48, optional)
1 pound Fontina, melted (optional)

Thoroughly wash the spinach, until the water in the basin runs clear. Steam, uncovered, until tender, 8 to 10 minutes. Drain well. Puree the spinach in a food processor and measure out 6 cups.

Mix the spinach with the parmesan and salt and pepper to taste. Stir in the eggs.

Preheat the oven to 300° F. Thickly butter a 6-cup ring mold or a 10-inch loaf pan.

Fill the mold or pan with the spinach mixture and tap on the counter to make it settle. Smooth the top. Dot with butter.

Bake for 50 minutes, until a skewer inserted in the center comes out clean.

Remove the sformato from the oven and let it stand for 10 minutes, then unmold it onto a serving platter. If you used a ring mold, fill the center with the piselli or the carciofi, if desired, placing any remaining peas or artichokes around the edges. If using a loaf pan, you can spoon the melted cheese on top, letting it run down the sides. This mold serves about 10 people.

In April and May my garden at Case Vecchie is covered with wild chard, which looks like the small cultivated kind but has a stronger flavor. This is the chard I like best of all, but I have to fight to keep it because it is considered a weed. I would prefer my garden to be a little more wild sometimes, but Vincenzo Curcio, who is in charge of all matters pertaining to the land at Regaleali, wants it to be trim and tidy like the vineyards.

Wild Greens

We country-bred Sicilians like to use all that nature has to offer in the way of good food in every season. Various other kinds of wild greens—some bitter, others not—are gathered in the countryside after a rain.

Often the most unusual and rarest of food plants are available only to the very poor, who know when and where to pick them. People used to bring special wild greens to our house on festive occasions or simply as a gesture of friendship. I still remember my grandfather savoring with great relish a gift of wild asparagus. We children hated it because it was so bitter, but he and other members of the family who really knew about food appreciated its worth.

Wild greens are usually cooked and served plain, with olive oil or with olive oil and vinegar or lemon juice added at the table; cheese—usually *tuma* (curd cheese) or *primo sale* (young pecorino) and grated parmesan—is served, too. At Regaleali we are lucky that we are able to have freshly made, still-warm ricotta with our greens. Sometimes the cooked greens are chopped and sautéed with garlic in olive oil, then seasoned with ground hot pepper. We call this dish *Verdura Salata con Aglio, Olio, e Peperoncino.* Greens like our wild greens may be hard to find outside Sicily, but you could certainly prepare other kinds, such as mustard greens or escarole or *broccoletto di rapa,* this way.

Some of the more bitter greens, such as *cavolicelli di montagna* (mountain cabbage) and wild asparagus, are used to make sauce for pasta. You could also make this *Pasta con la Verdura Amara* with *broccoletto di rapa.*

All greens—wild or not—have to be trimmed and washed thoroughly in several changes of cold water to get all the earth out; then they should be boiled until tender. We always leave the pot uncovered; that way the greens don't lose their bright color and strong flavor.

PASTA CON LA VERDURA AMARA *Pasta with Bitter Greens*

1 1/2 cups cooked greens (about 3 pounds fresh)
1 garlic clove, finely chopped
1/4 cup olive oil
Salt
Black pepper
2 tablespoons butter
1 1/2 pounds spaghetti
1/2 cup grated pecorino or parmesan

Coarsely chop the greens. Sauté the garlic in the olive oil until just golden, 1 to 2 minutes. Stir in the greens, season to taste with salt and pepper, and mix well. Put the butter in the bottom of a large serving dish.

Cook the spaghetti in boiling salted water until al dente. Drain, transfer to the serving dish, and toss to coat with the butter. Toss with some of the greens and cover with the rest. Sprinkle with some of the grated cheese and pass the rest of the cheese at the table. Serve this immediately; it serves 6 as a first course.

Asparagus

The Sicilian asparagus (*Ruscus hypoglossum*) is unlike that commonly cultivated for food in continental Europe or North America (*Asparagus officinalis*). The plant is barely two feet high, with dark-green shiny leaves similar to those of bay; its fruit is a tiny red berry. These *asparagi di giardino* (garden asparagus) are often used as a decorative border in private homes or old cloister gardens. The edible shoot is very thin and has a distinctive taste, not quite so bitter as the wild asparagus.

The most common way to eat asparagus in Sicily is in *Insalata di Asparagi* (Asparagus Salad). You break off and discard the ends—even very thin asparagus can be tough at the bottom of the stalk—and cook the asparagus in boiling salted water until it's tender. (I test by pinching the stalk.) Drain and cool the asparagus, then put it in a bowl and dress it with olive oil. Some people like to add vinegar or lemon juice; of the two, I prefer lemon juice. Eat the salad with pieces of pecorino and bread for dipping.

TOP: *Wild greens grow in profusion at Regaleali. We sauté them and eat them plain or with pasta or fresh cheese.*
ABOVE: *Asparagus plants form a low evergreen hedge, very handsome in the flower garden.*

Salad Greens

You seldom see green salad on a Sicilian table; it is not really part of the Sicilian tradition. When we have guests, my mother does not put salad on the menu, and yet, I remember her always eating salads. My grandfather used to tease her, calling her *la capruzza* (little goat) because she ate raw vegetables instead of meat. She does put salad on the menu for family meals, though, invented combinations of whatever raw vegetables, and maybe apple, that she finds in the kitchen. As for Mario, the most he can think to do is tomato salad. Maybe a *monzù* is not supposed to make salad. Too lowly.

Nevertheless, we do plant salad greens in the vegetable garden at Regaleali, and I also plant them in my garden at Mondello, the seaside suburb of Palermo where I have a house. We order the seeds from a catalog, plant them, and keep them going by watering them every day.

We have essentially two kinds of lettuce, *lattuga romana,* which is similar to Boston or butterhead lettuce, and *lattuga nostrana*. Literally translated as "our kind of lettuce," *lattuga nostrana* is the lettuce just about every Sicilian plants and eats. It has a long, narrow, jagged leaf with a rather large rib, and it is very crisp and juicy. We often serve the leaves after a spicy dish or barbecue to refresh the palate—as chic people at a chic dinner party would do with a sorbet. They are very good in salad. We also put purslane in salads, particularly with tomatoes. It grows as a weed in my garden in Mondello, so I just don't pull it all out. Arugula, an "import" from mainland Italy that I like, has to be planted if I want to have some.

When I was first married, I lived with my husband's family in Palermo. They had lived everywhere in Europe and were quite cosmopolitan in their habits, and they, too, had a *monzù*. My father-in-law, whom I dearly loved, was one of those aristocrats who didn't know how to boil an egg himself but definitely knew how to tell his *monzù* the correct way to make a soufflé. In fact, in those days we had the most wonderful soufflés you can imagine, creamy inside and filled with all sorts of things, from angel-hair pasta to poached eggs. We never had a meal at my in-laws' without a green salad to accompany the *pièce forte* (main course) and a cooked vegetable to follow. But this was quite unusual then, and even now, though you see more salads lately since people have become so concerned about their health.

I decided to put salad definitively on the menu at Regaleali one day when we had a Canadian visitor who had been touring Sicily. He said he was pleased with what he had had to eat, but, he asked me, "Why are so few vegetables served?" Indeed! It was May, and you could find an abundance of vegetables and greens everywhere but on the table.

My mother wasn't at home, so I was in charge. I took a basket of greens and oranges downstairs to the little kitchen, where Mario doesn't go—to tell you how much I dreaded his scorn. His assistant, Salvatore Campisi, was there, though, and when he saw me, he started shaking his head and gesturing in that special way Sicilians have. "Who do you think is going to eat this?" he asked. The look on his face would have discouraged anyone else, but I washed the salad and made the dressing just the same. Then I had to leave the kitchen to be with my guests, so Salvatore was obliged to toss the salad himself. There was an enormous amount, but it was all devoured.

From that day on, we've always had salad on the table. My two favorites are *Insalata Verde Mista con Menta* (Green Salad with Mint), greens with thinly sliced red onions and mint leaves, and *Insalata Verde Mista con gli Agrumi*, which is what we had that memorable day. Both are dressed with a mixture of grapefruit, orange, and lemon juice (whatever I have on hand), vinegar, and olive oil.

INSALATA VERDE MISTA CON GLI AGRUMI *Green Salad with Citrus*

6 cups mixed salad greens
$^1/_2$ grapefruit
1 blood orange
$^1/_4$ cup olive oil
2 to 3 tablespoons vinegar
Salt
Black pepper
1 teaspoon finely chopped shallot

Thoroughly wash and dry the greens and put them into a salad bowl. Peel the grapefruit and orange, separate into segments over a small bowl, and squeeze the membranes to get every drop of juice. Put the segments in the bowl with the juice and add the olive oil, vinegar, and salt and pepper to taste. Stir in the shallot. Pour over the greens and toss. This refreshing salad serves 4.

While we are enjoying the first fresh vegetables of the new year, the inexorable rhythms of agricultural life go on. In April, the tomato seeds, carefully saved from last year's crop, are sown in the corner of the field where they are to be grown and covered with plastic sheeting to protect them and keep them warm. The tomato seed is very delicate, especially when it first germinates. Every day the sheets are rolled back, and the seedlings are watered by hand with a watering can. When the seedlings are strong enough, they are transplanted. Then insects, rain, and hail are the enemies.

The earth is prepared for a new vineyard under the watchful eye of Vincenzo Curcio.

Wine

In the vineyards, meanwhile, the earth is being turned. A cultivator drawn by a small tractor goes up and down between the rows of vines, but the foot of the vine is tended by hand with the *zappa*, the same type of hoe that was used in my grandfather's time. Sometimes nothing can improve on the ways of the past. The canes are tied with colored plastic ribbons to the wires of the trellises. Most of our vines are espaliered, though some are head-trained. This traditional Sicilian way of training vines is called *alberello*. The vines seem to sleep as they wait for the kiss of sunshine to make them flourish again.

Regaleali has always had success with wine. The earliest record of grape growing goes back more than four hundred years to a 1580 document that refers to the vineyard of "Rekaliali." Located in central Sicily on the thirty-seventh parallel, the land is high (one hundred fifty to two hundred feet above sea level) and hilly and benefits from the *tramontana*, a north wind that cools the hot afternoons of summer. It is very dry.

In the 1920s, wine production got a big boost when my grandfather Lucio Tasca Bordonaro planted new vineyards and expanded the cellars. The quality of the wine was improved, and villagers and merchants came by cart or by mule and donkey to fill their barrels at the winery. Once the road to Regaleali was built, in 1950, demand increased even further.

Lucio's eldest son, Giuseppe, supervises the planting of a new vineyard

Wine making always fascinated my father. When he took full control of Regaleali after my grandfather's death in 1957, he began to dream of bottling the wine and making it famous far beyond the neighboring villages, beyond the shores of Sicily, even beyond Italy and Europe. He saw it as a way to make Regaleali pay for itself in an era when many landowners were suddenly finding they had to practice a profession in order to support the land, instead of the other way around, as it had been in the past.

It was no longer economical to grow wheat or any of the old crops. The fertile clay-and-limestone soil of Regaleali, however, was ideal for growing grapes. My father concentrated on wine making. He extended the vineyards and little by little began to realize his dream of bottling and selling Regaleali wine outside Sicily.

The first bottled wine was sold in 1966, but it proved to have a short bottle life, which was a great disappointment. My father had to find out if it was worth continuing with the wine or if he should look for some other way to keep Regaleali going. He consulted the now-legendary enologist Ezio Rivella. Rivella offered a lot of sound advice on how to stabilize the wines and recommended his right-hand man, Lorenzo Peira. Peira is now our most trusted adviser in whatever concerns the winery. He comes often and stays with us. Since 1968, we also have a full-time enologist, Giuseppe Cavaleri, working at the winery. He is *direttore di vinificazione,* and he has an apartment at the Case Grandi, the central farmhouse, where my parents live. It is right next door to the winery.

During the early years, my mother sold the wine. Drawing on her prodigious energy and charm, she went from restaurant to restaurant, persuading the owners to put Regaleali wines on their tables and on their wine lists. She sold 80,000 bottles in 1967 and 130,000 in 1968. Then in 1969 my parents met Ignazio Miceli, whose family had a wineshop. He was a young man looking for a way to make his fortune. He believed in our wines from the beginning and now distributes them worldwide.

In the early 1980s we greatly expanded the winery. Only the cellar, called *la bottaia vecchia* (the old barrelhouse), has kept its old look. But in making changes, we were very careful not to change the outward appearance of the old buildings. It is the look we are used to, and we want to keep it. In fact, arriving at the Case Grandi, you wouldn't imagine that there is a modern winery in the back.

Credit for these new developments is shared by my father and my brother, Lucio, who now runs the winery. His son Giuseppe, who holds a university degree in agronomy, also lives and works at Regaleali. Like our father before him, Lucio started by growing his own grapes on a small parcel of land. Since 1981, he has gradually taken over the management of the winery, bringing to it a somewhat different approach than my father's but the same love of the land and of Regaleali.

It was Lucio's idea to change the barrels from chestnut to French oak, which he feels produces wine that is better suited to the modern palate. All of us had an opinion, as usual. My father was very attached to the chestnut, but Lucio insisted, and my father finally gave in. Now he admits that the wines aged in oak taste better than the ones aged in chestnut. The old barrels did not go to waste—my mother had them cut in half and planted them with wild roses to fill in the open spaces around the winery.

The Feast of San Giuseppe

We mark the official beginning of spring on March 19 with a big celebration of the feast of San Giuseppe, which is also my father's name day. Since it is his special day, we all try to be at Regaleali. It gives my father enormous pleasure to sit at the table surrounded by all the people he loves. The house is filled with family and friends, and those who are too far away to join us call with their good wishes.

On the eve of the feast day, we build the traditional bonfire in the yard of the winery. It is a huge fire, and the flames leap so high they light the buildings as bright as day. It is a kind of purification rite, I suppose, this burning of all that is old. For those who live in the country, spring is always a new beginning.

In keeping with the tradition of making bread in fanciful shapes on the feast of San Giuseppe, we decorate the table at the Case Grandi with long breadsticks that we keep until they crumble. They used to be sprinkled with sesame and poppy seeds, but since the cultivation of poppies has been outlawed, we now use only sesame seed, *giuggiulena,* as it is called in dialect. Some farmers grow poppies even though it is illegal to do so. I discovered this one summer when I went to Mass in Vallelunga, the village closest to Regaleali, on the feast of San Calogero. I had been told the observances on that day were particularly interesting, and indeed they were. People brought ex-votos made of bread covered with poppy seeds to church to be blessed. They shaped the loaves of bread according to what ailed them—an arm, a leg, a head—I even saw one made in the shape of a child. After the blessing, the ex-votos were distributed to the faithful.

When I was a little girl, the family of one of our employees whose son was called Piddu (short for Giuseppe in dialect) used to do the traditional home altar that is adorned with flowers and ornamental breads. Only they made special breads—no one at Regaleali has done them since—and they decorated their table with *bastoni di San Giuseppe* (hollyhocks). These flowers grow all over Sicily; if you plant them once, they will live forever. San Giuseppe, one story goes, walked with a real *bastone* (staff), which God made burst into bloom to prove to a nonbeliever that Joseph was a saint.

Among all his many roles and attributes, San Giuseppe is the patron saint of fruit vendors. You will see his portrait hanging in the stalls in the Vucciria, the open-air market in Palermo, and elsewhere. We have a portrait of him—the classic one, with him holding a lily, the symbol of purity, in his hand—that we put on the bower we build when we eat outside with a lot of people.

The traditional dishes for the feast of San Giuseppe are *Pasta con le Sarde* and *macco* (dried fava puree), a thick puree flavored with wild fennel and borage. It is more or less the same recipe as for *Minestra delle Ultime Fave,* but it is cooked longer. At Regaleali, as in the rest of Sicily, we must have *Sfince di San Giuseppe* filled with *Crema di Ricotta.* They are served as dessert. Some people prefer not to fill the *sfince* but to roll them in sugar or honey and serve them warm. Either way, everybody eats *sfince* on this day.

I knew ricotta would cause problems when my recipes were tested in the United States. Our sheep's milk ricotta has a much richer, saltier flavor than any I have found there. Then one day when I was in a grocery store near Washington, D.C., I saw a piece of ricotta salata in the cheese case. It gave me the idea of mixing some in for the dessert dishes using ricotta. About a half pound of crumbled ricotta salata to one pound of ricotta turned out to be right. The flavored ricotta was not as salty as ours, nor did it have the same texture, but the taste was close. Pure serendipity! This is what we used for the *Crema di Ricotta* that goes in the *sfince, Cassata, Cannoli,* and *Torta di Ricotta con Canditi.*

SFINCE DI SAN GIUSEPPE *Saint Joseph's Cream Puffs*

Pâte à Choux

1 cup water

5 tablespoons butter, cut into ¹/₂-inch dice

Pinch of salt

1 cup flour, sifted

4 eggs, at room temperature

⊷

Oil, for frying

1¹/₂ cups Crema di Ricotta (recipe follows), mixed with 1 tablespoon chopped candied fruit

Candied orange peel, for garnish

To make the pâte à choux, pour the water into a medium saucepan, add the butter and salt, and bring to a boil. Add the flour all at once, remove from the heat, and stir constantly until the dough comes off the sides of the pan. Turn the dough out onto a cool surface or into a bowl to cool. When the dough has cooled, add the eggs, one by one, stirring to blend thoroughly.

Heat about 2 to 3 inches of oil to 350°F. in a medium saucepan or deep fryer. There must be enough oil to allow the dough to roll over and swell to about 3 times its original size when it is cooking. Drop 1 rounded teaspoon of dough into the hot oil, using your finger to push the dough from the spoon. Do not crowd the pot. The sfince will cook, tripling in size, in about 3 minutes. Be sure to turn the sfince and brown them on the other side. Drain the sfince on brown paper and let them cool.

Using a pastry bag fitted with the small tip, fill the sfince with the crema mixture. Garnish with a piece of candied orange peel. This makes enough sfince for 8.

Sfince for all on the feast of San Giuseppe.

CREMA DI RICOTTA *Ricotta Cream*

³/₄ pound ricotta (about 1¹/₂ cups), preferably skim milk (see page 22)
¹/₄ cup sugar

Make this the day before you will use it.

Drain the ricotta by placing it in a strainer set in a bowl. Refrigerate for at least 2 to 3 hours, preferably overnight.

Put the drained ricotta in a food processor and process until smooth. Transfer the ricotta to a mixing bowl, add the sugar, and whip by hand or with an electric mixer until light and fluffy. Cover this and refrigerate it until you are ready to use it. This makes about 1¹/₂ cups of crema, enough to fill the Sfince di San Giuseppe.

Bread

The bread for the feast of San Giuseppe is baked in the wood-burning oven that we kept when we installed a modern kitchen at Case Vecchie for my cooking classes. Until the late forties, bread was baked there every day. Then bread was part of the farm workers' daily pay, along with a liter of wine and other country products, often including *Sarde Salata*. But now the workers are paid cash, and even my parents prefer the bread from the bakery in town.

Bread, homemade or not, is still the favorite food—a holy food, I would say—of all Sicilians. A Sicilian will not sit down at the table unless it is set with bread to go with everything—pasta, cheese, tomatoes, onions, eggplant, even grapes. Any excuse is good enough for a bite of bread.

The idea of eating bread made from freshly milled grain that was sown and reaped on your own land is a very powerful one. In his novel *The Leopard*, set in late-nineteenth-century Sicily, Giuseppe di Lampedusa describes a house in a village near Palermo: "[A]nother corner of the room was bounded by high stiff matting, hiding the honey-colored wheat taken weekly to the mill for the family's needs."

In the old days, there was one person who did nothing but bake bread. He would bring our wheat from the granary to the village water mill to be ground by stone. The miller would take the grain and a short while later hand back a sack of fine whole wheat semolina flour. A few of these mills still stand in Sicily, but most have been replaced by machines.

Now Carmelo Di Martino, who lives at Case Vecchie, bakes the bread, but only for special occasions. According to Carmelo, bread is no good unless it is made from flour ground the old-fashioned way. He will travel miles to find a mill with a stone grindstone, then bring the flour home and sift it himself to separate the bran, which used to be set aside to make *canigghiotti* (bread for dogs). Imagine!

Liboria, Carmelo's wife, used to bake the bread. Then one day she had to go to the village to take care of her elderly mother. We were expecting visitors, and I had planned to serve them freshly baked bread. Carmelo assured me that he knew how to make it, but I was suspicious—a Sicilian will never tell you he doesn't know how to do something. Carmelo's been making the bread ever since, and his bread is even better than Liboria's—crisp, firm, yellow on the inside, with a dark crust and fragrance that recall bygone days.

All that it has in it is *farina rimacinata*, that is, twice-milled semolina flour, *crescente* (starter), some additional yeast, salt, and water—nothing else. It is made in the *madia*, the wooden trough traditionally used for bread dough. Carmelo works the dough, punching it with his fists and kneading it with a twist of the wrist, for thirty, thirty-five minutes. The longer the dough is worked, the better the bread. Then he forms the loaves, places them on a blanket spread with a clean cloth, covers them with a doubled quilt, and leaves them for at least three hours (exactly how long depends on the outside temperature), until they are ready to bake. "With heat," he says, "the fever comes," explaining how the loaves rise between the bed covers.

He always makes some *fruata*, as he calls it (I would call it *focaccia*), a small, almost-hollow loaf somewhat like a pita. Fresh from the oven, still hot, and dipped in a mixture of oil, salt, and oregano, this is food fit for the gods.

Sometimes when we have bread dough on hand, we make *Cudduruni* (Fried Bread Dough with Honey) for dessert. You should try it sometime. Let some of the dough rise a little more than for bread, then cut it into small pieces. Press them down and deep-fry them. Drain on brown paper and coat them with honey. If you think they're too sweet, they're probably just right.

Carmelo makes ten two-pound loaves of bread at a time; he says it's not worth firing the oven for fewer than that. Indeed, it takes about an hour and a half for the fire to be ready, for the oven to be "white," as we say. My version of *Pane di Carmelo* is more manageable, and you can bake the bread in a home oven—there are fewer loaves, and the dough takes less time to rise.

The fire burns down as Carmelo makes bread. He combines semolina flour, starter, and water in a wooden madia, then kneads the dough with his fists. He forms some large and some small loaves and leaves them to rise

on a well-worn cotton cloth. Tiny cracks on the surface tell him the loaves are ready to put in the oven. The bread comes out brown and crusty on the outside and yellow within. It smells heavenly.

PANE DI CARMELO *Semolina Bread*

10 cups semolina flour (about 4 pounds)
2 tablespoons salt
2 cakes compressed yeast or 2 packages dry yeast
4 to 4¹/₂ cups warm water
5 tablespoons olive oil
¹/₄ cup unhulled sesame seeds

Pour 9 cups of the flour onto a work surface or into a large bowl, mix in the salt, and make a well. Add the yeast (crumble in the yeast cakes) and add about 3 cups of the water. Begin working the dough with your hands or a wooden spoon to mix in the water. Once most of the water is absorbed, start kneading the dough. Add up to 1¹/₂ cups more water to the dough by pouring it on the work surface little by little and working the dough until it absorbs it. Semolina dough holds a lot of moisture, so the dough will feel more moist and sticky than other doughs. If the dough gets too wet, add as much of the remaining flour as necessary to form a smooth dough. Knead the dough for 30 to 35 minutes, folding it over and over itself. Add 2 to 3 tablespoons of the olive oil to the dough in the last 2 to 3 minutes of kneading. When the dough is smooth and elastic, it is ready. Cut the dough into 4 or 8 pieces, depending on what size loaf you want, and set aside.

Lightly sprinkle two 12×18-inch baking sheets with semolina flour and set aside.

Pour some olive oil on the surface where you have been kneading the bread and sprinkle it with sesame seeds. Place each piece of dough on top of the oil and seeds and roll and shape it into a round loaf. Set the loaves on the prepared baking sheets. Cover them with a clean kitchen cloth and set them in a warm place to rise until nearly double, about 45 minutes to 1 hour. The loaves are ready to bake when there are tiny cracks on the surface of the dough.

Preheat the oven to 375°F.

Bake the bread for 50 minutes to 1 hour, until the loaves are golden and firm to the touch. Cool them on a wire rack. This makes 4 large or 8 small loaves.

Wherever you go in Italy, you will find a different kind of bread. Every locality, even the smallest little place in the countryside, has its own special loaf. Palermo is known to have very good bread, which is not surprising, since wheat was such an important crop in Sicily for so long and since much of that grain passed through the port of Palermo.

In Mondello, the baker comes around every morning at eleven, heralded by all the dogs in the neighborhood. His creaky old red van lets the whole world know the bread has arrived. He goes up to the door, rings the bell, and hands you a loaf, announcing *"Pane!"* in his booming voice. And what wonderful bread it is, warm and aromatic and covered with sesame seeds. Since it is made of hard wheat, it stays good for at least two days. If any is left, we save it for breadcrumbs.

‖ *Breadcrumbs* ‖

I never paid much attention to breadcrumbs, and when I watched Mario using them in my mother's kitchen, it never occurred to me that his breadcrumbs were any different from anyone else's. Then one day we were working in Ann Yonkers's kitchen in Washington. We were making *Braciolettine* for a party and were about to bread them. Suddenly I noticed Ann offering Mario all sorts of breadcrumbs as he turned them down one by one—these are not fine enough, those are not even enough, these are made from mixed whole wheat and white bread, and so on. He had to use Ann's breadcrumbs, but the next day he went to get some from an Italian restaurant kitchen where he felt certain they would have the right kind.

For Mario, the only proper breadcrumbs come from plain hard-wheat bread that is dried, then finely crushed and sifted. While it is true that breadcrumbs are an important ingredient in Sicilian cooking, I wouldn't be as particular about them as Mario is, except to say that you shouldn't keep them too long in the cupboard.

At home Mario often makes *Braciolettine* for us to take on a picnic or to eat cold with a salad for supper on Sunday. You can make the little meat rolls and thread them on double skewers ahead of time and bake them just before serving.

BRACIOLETTINE *Meat Rolls*

Ripieno

1 onion, finely chopped

2 tablespoons olive oil

¼ pound Gruyère, cut into tiny cubes

¼ pound boiled ham, cut into tiny cubes

½ cup chopped parsley

3 egg yolks, beaten

1 cup cubed bread, with cubes cut tiny, ¼ inch

Salt

Black pepper

↔

1½ to 2 pounds top round of beef or leg of lamb, sliced very thin (⅛ inch)

Seven ½-inch-thick slices dense Italian bread or dense sandwich bread (about 1 pound),
  crusts removed

20 bay leaves, soaked in hot water if brittle

2 onions, cut into 1-inch wedges

6 tablespoons olive oil

2 to 3 cups fine breadcrumbs

To make the ripieno, sauté the chopped onion in the olive oil until just golden, 2 to 3 minutes. Remove the sautéed onion from the heat and let it cool. Add the Gruyère, ham, parsley, egg yolks, and bread cubes and mix well. Season to taste with salt and pepper and set aside.

If necessary, pound the meat until it is ⅛ inch thick. Cut the meat into 3-inch squares. Put about 1 scant tablespoon of stuffing on each slice of meat, near one of the corners. Roll the corner of the meat over the stuffing, tuck in the edges, and roll it into a small sausagelike shape, about 1 inch thick by 2½ to 3 inches long. Continue until all are done.

Cut the bread slices into pieces about the same size as the meat rolls.

Preheat the oven to 350°F. Oil a baking pan and sprinkle it with salt.

Thread 2 bamboo skewers through the side of a meat roll. Add a bay leaf, a wedge of onion, and a piece of bread. Repeat to fill all the skewers. Pour the olive oil into one large flat dish and the breadcrumbs into another. Dip the skewers in the olive oil and then in breadcrumbs, coating them completely.

Arrange the skewers in the pan and bake for 20 to 25 minutes, turning once after 10 minutes. The Braciolettine are cooked when the meat is slightly browned

Two-pronged Sicilian skewers hold the Braciolettine in place.

and the stuffing is cooked through. Braciolettine are equally good hot or at room temperature.

This makes 10 to 14 Braciolettine, depending upon how much meat you use and how thin you pound it. This will serve 4 to 6 people as a main course.

In Sicily, virtually all our fried dishes are breaded, as are some baked ones, such as *Sgombri al Forno con Pane Grattato e Capperi* (Baked Breaded Mackerel with Capers). In this dish, mackerel (or sardines) are butterflied—that is, split open with the backbone and head removed but the tail left on—and steeped in vinegar for thirty minutes. Then the fish are drained, dipped in a mix of breadcrumbs, salt, pepper, and dried oregano, placed on an oiled baking dish, sprinkled with capers, and drizzled with olive oil. They go in a 350°F. oven for about twenty-five minutes and are served hot.

Breadcrumbs are actually used a lot with fish, as a stuffing for *Sarde a Beccafico* and *Involtini di Pesce Spada,* and as a garnish with fish-and-pasta dishes. These are dishes on which we do not put grated cheese; many Sicilians like to sprinkle them with toasted breadcrumbs so that the pasta is not too slippery. Some say the breadcrumb garnish makes a more satisfying mouthful.

Canned Fish

The classic fish dish on which we put breadcrumbs is *Pasta con Acciuga e Mollica* (Pasta with Anchovy and Breadcrumbs). For a pound of spaghetti (enough for four people), sauté a chopped small onion and a chopped garlic clove in three tablespoons of olive oil. Add six canned anchovy fillets and cook just until they melt. Remove from the heat. The anchovy fillets must not cook. If—and only if—tomatoes are in season, add a tomato, peeled, seeded, and cut into small cubes. If not, sprinkle the finished dish with plenty of chopped parsley and drizzle with olive oil. Pass a bowl of toasted breadcrumbs at the table for garnish. Be sure to use either the tomato or the parsley in the dish. Aside from their fresh taste, they make the dish look more appetizing; otherwise it is all brown.

Any number of wonderful fish-and-pasta dishes can be made from such ingredients as you are likely to have in the pantry. Among those we make with canned tuna are *Pasta con il Tonno Rosso* and *Pasta con il Tonno in Bianco*. Although we always have some of Mario's homemade preserved tuna on hand, we don't like to mix it with other ingredients; it's too good for that. Instead, we use albacore tuna packed in olive oil, but we rinse off the oil. (If you can't find albacore tuna, substitute solid white tuna packed in oil.) For the sauce we use our own olive oil, which tastes so much better.

PASTA CON IL TONNO ROSSO *Pasta with Tuna in Tomato Sauce*

2 cups *Salsa Pic-Pac* (page 110) or *Salsa di Pomodoro Passata* (page 114)

One 6½-ounce can albacore tuna packed in olive oil, rinsed and drained

¼ cup olive oil

Salt

Black pepper

1 pound spaghetti

3 tablespoons chopped parsley

¼ cup toasted breadcrumbs, for garnish (optional)

Heat the salsa in a medium saucepan and add the tuna and olive oil. Bring to a simmer and cook just until the sauce is heated through. Season with salt and pepper to taste. Set aside.

Cook the spaghetti in boiling salted water until al dente. Drain and transfer to a serving bowl. Pour half the sauce over the pasta and toss. Pour the rest on top. Garnish with parsley and breadcrumbs, if desired. Serve this at once. This serves 4 if you are very hungry, 6 if you are not.

Pasta con il Tonno in Bianco *Pasta with Tuna*

1 small onion, finely chopped

1 garlic clove, minced

1/2 cup olive oil

2 tablespoons white wine

1/4 cup chopped parsley

One 6 1/2-ounce can albacore tuna packed in olive oil, rinsed and drained

1 pound linguine

Ground hot pepper

Salt

Black pepper

1/2 cup toasted breadcrumbs, for garnish

Sauté the onion and garlic in half of the olive oil for 2 to 3 minutes, or until just golden. Stir in the wine and remove the mixture from the heat. Add the parsley, tuna, and the rest of the oil. Set aside.

Cook the linguine in boiling salted water until al dente. Reserve some of the cooking water in case you need to thin the sauce. Drain the linguine and toss with half of the sauce. Pour the remaining sauce on top of the pasta. Serve immediately with ground hot pepper, salt, black pepper, and breadcrumbs on the table. This serves 4 as a first course.

Another good pasta dish with tuna is *Pasta con Tonno e Acciughe* (Pasta with Tuna and Anchovies). For this, you sauté a chopped small onion and a chopped garlic clove in three tablespoons of olive oil, add a tablespoonful of water, and remove from the heat. Rinse, drain, and flake a can of albacore or white tuna packed in olive oil (6 1/2-ounce size), and add the tuna to the onion mixture. Add six canned anchovies, cut into small pieces, and a quarter cup of chopped parsley. In summer I also add a cup of peeled, seeded, and chopped tomatoes. Mix and season to taste with ground hot pepper, freshly ground black pepper, and salt. Stir in two tablespoons of olive oil. Cook a pound of dried linguine in boiling salted water until al dente and drain. Toss with most of the tuna-and-anchovy sauce, put the rest on top, and serve immediately. Pass toasted breadcrumbs in a bowl at the table. This amount will serve four to six people, depending on how hungry they are.

In the past even fish had seasons, and the fishermen had to wait upon their migrations. Spring was the time for both tuna and swordfish to pass close to the shores of Sicily. Nowadays such fish are in the market at other times of the year as well, but when the swordfish is ultrafresh, Mario is sure to prepare *Pesce Spada al Forno* with an herb sauce with some big capers from Pantelleria.

PESCE SPADA AL FORNO *Baked Swordfish with Herbs and Capers*

1 1/2 pounds swordfish, in 1 thick piece

1 medium onion, thickly sliced

2 garlic cloves, cut into pieces

1 tablespoon rosemary needles

1 tablespoon dried oregano

1/2 cup mint leaves

Salt

Black pepper

1 tablespoon butter

1/4 cup olive oil

1 cup white wine

Salsa a Parte

2 to 3 tablespoons red wine vinegar

1/2 teaspoon sugar

2 tablespoons freshly squeezed lemon juice

1/4 cup olive oil

1 garlic clove, minced

1 tablespoon dried oregano

1 tablespoon chopped parsley

2 tablespoons chopped mixed herbs, such as mint, rosemary, and thyme

1 tablespoon capers, rinsed

Salt

Black pepper

Olive trees and vineyards.

Preheat the oven to 375°F. Lightly grease a baking dish with olive oil.

Place the swordfish in the dish and surround with the onion and garlic. Season with the rosemary, oregano, and mint. Add salt and pepper to taste. Dot with bits of butter and drizzle with the olive oil. Bake for 10 minutes, then pour in the wine. Continue to bake until done, using the general guide of 10 minutes per 1-inch thickness of fish. Test by inserting the tip of a knife to see if the swordfish is tender.

While the fish is cooking, make the salsa. Stir the vinegar and sugar together in a small bowl to dissolve the sugar. Then add the lemon juice, olive oil, garlic, oregano, parsley, and other chopped herbs. Stir in the capers. Add salt and pepper to taste.

When the fish is done, transfer it to a serving platter and spoon the pan juices on top. Stir the salsa and pour some over the fish. Pass the rest at the table. This serves 4 as a main course.

In season or not, tuna appears frequently on the table. I love *Tonno al Forno* (Baked Tuna). The fish is stuffed as for *Tonno al Ragù,* but baked. If any is left over, it is flaked and mixed in with the pan juices and used as a sauce for spaghetti. For both *Tonno al Forno* and *Tonno al Ragù,* Mario uses a big piece of fish, at least two pounds, preferably from the tail, which he believes is the best part because "it exercises most." For *Tonna al Ragù* the fish is served covered with sauce and garnished with a bunch of mint. It, too, is delicious with the fish flaked and mixed in the sauce for pasta. Remember not to eat too much tuna at dinner; it is very heavy and will give you nightmares.

TONNO AL RAGÙ *Tuna Ragù*

2 pounds tuna, in 1 piece

2 garlic cloves, peeled

¼ cup mint leaves

Salt

Black pepper

1 large onion, chopped

¼ cup olive oil

1 heaping tablespoon Estratto di Pomodoro (see page 115) or 3 tablespoons sun-dried
  tomato paste

1 cup white wine

2 cups water

2 cups Salsa di Pomodoro Passata (page 114)

1 teaspoon sugar

2 bay leaves

Sprigs of mint, for garnish (optional)

Make slits in the tuna. Chop the garlic and mint together and stuff the mixture into the slits. Sprinkle the tuna with salt and pepper and any leftover garlic-mint mixture. Set aside.

Sauté the onion in the olive oil. Dissolve the estratto in the wine, then add it to the onion. Stir in the water, salsa, sugar, and bay leaves. Add more salt and pepper to taste. Simmer for 30 minutes, uncovered. Add the tuna and cook for 30 minutes longer over low heat.

Put the fish on a serving platter, spoon the sauce on top, and garnish with sprigs of mint, if desired. This serves 4 as a main course.

Ragù is the quintessential Sicilian tomato sauce. In fact, when a Sicilian talks about *pasta al sugo*, he means pasta with *ragù* sauce, not just any tomato sauce as *sugo* is understood in the rest of Italy. *Ragù* can be made with several different kinds of meat or fish—tuna, as just mentioned; pork and sausage; pigeon; lamb—or without.

I had been reading about lamb *ragù* and then in one of those strange coincidences that occur in life saw lamb *ragù* with pasta on the menu soon afterward at the restaurant in Gangivecchio, a remote and mysterious place in the mountains, not far from Regaleali. The restaurant is housed in an old monastery, and the owners prepare traditional Sicilian dishes, using what they grow or raise on their own land. It was the first time I had ever tasted lamb *ragù*, and I found it delicious.

Poultry

We raise a lot of poultry at Regaleali—chickens, turkeys, ducks, geese, and pigeons. My father used to like to see the geese walking around Case Vecchie; he even had a straw hut built in the courtyard for them to spend the night there. But whenever anyone passed by, they would all start honking. No wonder they saved the Capitoline in Rome from the enemy! I had to beg my father to move them away from my bedroom window.

Pigeons make a fantastic *ragù*. Our pigeons are quite small, but you can make the *Piccioni al Ragù* with squab. If you have any left over, remove the meat from the bones and reheat it in the sauce for pasta.

PICCIONI AL RAGÙ *Pigeon Ragù*

Four ³/₄-pound pigeons or squabs, cut in half through the breastbone

2 sprigs rosemary

2 sprigs thyme

2 bay leaves

¹/₂ cup olive oil

Salt

Black pepper

¹/₂ cup finely chopped onion

1 garlic clove, chopped

¹/₄ cup white wine

1 tablespoon Estratto di Pomodoro (see page 115) or 3 tablespoons sun-dried tomato paste

1¹/₂ cups Salsa di Pomodoro Passata (page 114)

3 cups water

1 teaspoon sugar

Put the pigeons, skin side up, 1 sprig rosemary, 1 sprig thyme, and 1 bay leaf in a skillet large enough to hold them all in one layer. Cook over medium-high heat, turning the pigeons to dry them out. Add half of the oil and brown the pigeons. Season with salt and pepper to taste.

Meanwhile, sauté the onion and garlic in the rest of the olive oil in another pan, shaking from time to time, until just golden, 2 to 3 minutes. Stir in the wine, estratto, salsa, and water. Add the rest of the rosemary, the thyme, and bay leaf, the sugar, and salt and pepper to taste. Add the pigeons, cover, and simmer for 40 to 50 minutes, or until the meat is tender. Uncover and cook to reduce the sauce, about 10 minutes. Serve the pigeons in the sauce. This serves 4 as a main dish.

PICCIONI SUL CROSTONE *Pigeons on Toast*

Two 1-pound pigeons or squabs

¹/₄ cup olive oil

Salt

Black pepper

¹/₂ cup chopped pancetta

1 cup finely chopped red onion

³/₄ cup red wine

³/₄ cup water

4 slices sandwich bread, crusts removed, cut diagonally

2 tablespoons butter

4 chicken livers, cleaned and finely chopped

¹/₂ cup finely chopped prosciutto

¹/₄ cup finely chopped boiled ham

¹/₄ cup chopped parsley, for garnish

Brown the pigeons in the olive oil until they have a nice mahogany color. Season to taste with salt and pepper. Add the pancetta and ¹/₂ cup of the onion and cook briefly. Add ¹/₂ cup of the wine and all the water. Cover and cook over low heat for about 40 to 50 minutes, or until the meat is tender. You will have a very small amount of pan juice. When the pigeons are cooked, remove them from the pan and cut each one in half lengthwise, through the breast and backbone. Put them back in the pan and set aside in a warm place.

Toast the bread and put it in the oven to keep warm. Sauté the remaining onion in the butter for 2 to 3 minutes. Add the chicken livers, prosciutto, and boiled ham and cook the mixture until browned. Season to taste with salt and pepper. Add the remaining wine and cook until the mixture is thickened and takes on a puree consistency.

Remove the toast from the oven and spread it with the puree. Lay a half pigeon on top of each piece of toast and spoon some of the pan juice over. Garnish with parsley. This serves 4 as a second course, after any pasta dish you like.

With duck, Mario makes *Anatra in Salsa Suprema*, which is served in a ring of *Purea di Patate*. Most people love it, but I find the cream-and-brandy sauce too rich. Or maybe it's that I don't like duck meat or, for that matter, ducks. The breed we have is called *anatra muta* (dumb duck). The ducks don't quack; instead, they have a strangulated cry that is really pitiful.

The pigeon house at Case Vecchie.

ANATRA IN SALSA SUPREMA *Duck in Cognac Sauce*

One 5- to 6-pound duck
¹/₄ cup olive oil
1 medium onion, finely chopped
1 cup white wine
Salt
Black pepper
¹/₄ cup cognac
¹/₂ cup heavy cream
1 heaping tablespoon flour mixed with ¹/₂ cup water

Put the duck in a deep skillet, add the olive oil, and brown over medium heat. Pour out all but ¹/₄ cup grease from the pan. Add the onion and cook for 5 to 7 minutes. Add the wine and deglaze the pan. Cover and continue cooking, shaking and scraping the pan from time to time, until the duck is tender, about 30 to 40 minutes. Season to taste with salt and pepper.

Remove the duck from the pan. Discard the skin and cut the duck into 4 to 6 pieces. Set aside in a warm place. Deglaze the pan with the cognac, pass the pan juices through a food mill, and pour them into a small saucepan. Stir in the heavy cream. Add the flour-water slurry to the sauce. Cook the sauce until it thickens, then taste it and adjust the seasonings. Arrange the duck on a serving platter and pour some sauce on top. Pass the rest of the sauce in a sauceboat. This serves 4.

‖ ℒ a m b ‖

Lamb is the meat we eat most often, and the one I like best. We have a flock of about three hundred sheep at Regaleali, a breed called *testa rossa* (red head), which has a long, reddish-brown face. The lambs are born at the end of August, beginning of September, and almost every mature ewe has at least one. The healthier, sturdier ewes are more likely to have twins. If there is enough pasturage that year, we keep both; if not, one is given away or sold. The lambs are milk fed for about two months. It is always amusing to watch them, the way they stay together, run together, even sleep on top of one another. And then when one makes a decision, all the others follow.

At the beginning of November, the baby lambs are put out to pasture, and the milking of the ewes, which was suspended toward the end of their pregnant period, is resumed. Cheese making starts up again.

The ewes that were too young to breed earlier in the year are mated in the fall to deliver in March, in time for the Easter lamb. *Agnello al Forno*, which is roasted with rosemary, is the classic Sicilian way to prepare baby lamb. Some people are disturbed by the bones, but that's the way we like it. We find that the meat closest to the bone has the best flavor.

AGNELLO AL FORNO *Roast Lamb*

4 pounds baby lamb, cut up, or lamb shoulder chops, with bones, trimmed
Salt
Black pepper
¹/₃ cup rosemary needles
¹/₃ cup olive oil
1 red onion, sliced
1 cup red wine
Rosemary sprigs, for garnish

Preheat the oven to 400°F.

Season the lamb with salt, pepper, and rosemary. Coat with the olive oil and put the lamb in a roasting pan with the onion. Roast for 10 minutes, then add ¹/₂ cup of the wine. Continue roasting for another 20 to 25 minutes, then remove the pan from the oven and stir and turn the lamb. Add the remaining ¹/₂ cup of wine and roast for another 10 to 15 minutes. Put the lamb on a serving dish. Scrape the pan with a spatula, pour the juices on the lamb, and serve it hot, garnished with rosemary sprigs. This serves 6 to 8 as a main course.

With few exceptions, the lamb's life is not a happy one. While the lambs are still nursing, some are killed to take the stomachs for *caglio* (rennet), which will be needed later for the cheese. These very young lambs are the best to eat, and when one is killed, we are sure to have *Stigghiole* (Grilled Lamb Intestines). You get only five of these delicacies from each lamb, and it takes two to make a proper serving. When we were all living at home, we used to fight over the *Stigghiole*. Once we got a freezer, my mother thought she would have the intestines cleaned and frozen until there were enough to go around, but usually we couldn't wait.

No one can make *Stigghiole* like Carmelo. First he cleans the intestines and caul fat thoroughly. He spreads the caul fat out on the table and cuts five short pieces each of the duodenum and ileum, the two upper parts of the intestine, and five long pieces of the remaining section of intestine (what is used for casings in sausage making). He lines up the short pieces on the caul in five separate piles, puts a scallion and two sprigs of parsley on each, and sprinkles the piles with salt, black pepper, and grated pecorino cheese. Then Carmelo cuts the caul and wraps it around each little pile, takes a length of casing, and winds it tightly around each bundle until it is stiff like a stick. He does this by winding a strip first down then up the length of each bundle and tying the ends together at the top. *Stigghiole* are grilled over the coals. Delicious, but not for the squeamish.

When a young lamb is killed in spring, Mario is likely to make *Agnello in Fricassea*. It's hard to choose, but I think that if I had to, I would say that this is my favorite lamb dish. It is also a good example of French influence on the Sicilian *monzù* tradition.

Purea di Patate is perfect with the *fricassea*. We arrange the mashed potatoes in a ring on the serving dish to keep the juices from running off the plate and spoon the stew in the middle. We do this also with such other stewlike dishes as *Spezzato di Montone alla Menta*, *Castrato al Rosso del Conte*, and *Anatra in Salsa Suprema*. For *Pollo Conti d'Almerita* we usually make a ring of rice.

AGNELLO IN FRICASSEA *Lamb Fricassee*

4 pounds lamb stew meat with bones, or 3 pounds boneless shoulder or leg of lamb, well
*   trimmed and cut into 3- to 4-inch pieces*
2 medium onions, peeled
3 beef bouillon cubes
4 egg yolks
1 cup heavy cream
4 tablespoons butter, softened
Juice of 2 lemons
2 tablespoons flour mixed with 1/2 cup water
Salt
Black pepper
Chopped parsley, for garnish

Put the lamb and onions in a large pot. Add the bouillon cubes and water to
cover. Bring to a boil, reduce the heat, and cook, uncovered, until the lamb is very
tender, at least 45 minutes, but perhaps up to 1 hour and 15 minutes, depending on
the cut of meat.

Whisk together the egg yolks, cream, butter, and lemon juice in a small bowl.
Remove the meat from the broth. Arrange it on a large platter, cover it, and keep it
warm. Strain the broth and return it to the saucepan.

Whisk in the flour-water slurry and bring the broth to a boil for 2 to 3 minutes.
Reduce the heat and whisk in the egg mixture, stirring continuously until thickened,
about 10 minutes. Be careful not to boil the sauce, or it will curdle the eggs. Season
to taste with salt and pepper.

Ladle most of the sauce over the lamb and sprinkle with parsley. Pass the remaining sauce at the table. The lamb serves 6 to 8 as a main course.

Agnello in Fricassea reflects the French influence in monzù cooking. The high ceilings of the salon at Case Grandi are a reminder of its past as the granary. We gather here for family occasions.

PUREA DI PATATE *Mashed Potatoes*

4 pounds boiling potatoes, peeled
8 tablespoons butter
1 to 1 1/2 cups milk
3/4 cup grated parmesan (optional)
Salt

Cook the potatoes in salted water until tender. Drain and pass them through a food mill back into the cooking pot. Add the butter and stir. Stir in enough milk to lighten. Add the cheese, if you care to, and salt to taste. If you are not serving this immediately, pour a bit more milk on top to keep a crust from forming. Stir that milk in just before serving. This serves 6 to 8.

Most of the lambs, however, will join the flock, at least for a while. The best males will be saved for breeding, the others for eating. The best of the young females will be kept to replace the toothless old ewes who can't graze anymore. The male lambs are castrated at six months and killed at one year. This so-called *castrato* is what we mostly eat, and we eat a lot of it. The meat is cooked in many different ways. The ribs are grilled, the legs cut into pieces for stews or sliced for *Braciolettine,* and the bits and pieces ground for *polpette* (meatballs). The flavor of meat is, of course, influenced by an animal's diet as well as its age and sex. The best feeding for the sheep comes when they are let into the wheat fields after the harvest in late summer. After that, they are slaughtered. At that point they are also at the peak of their physical development.

The sheep are sheared by hand at the beginning of June, and they are quite a sight, so ugly and naked looking. Nobody wants to work the wool, which is very coarse, and it is almost impossible to sell it. My mother used to have the fleece washed and carded for stuffing mattresses and cushions, but no one wants to do that anymore. We will have to give up sleeping on wool. I also remember that until the war the women used to spin the wool to knit sweaters for their men. In those days they went to work on mules, and the sweaters kept them warm during the cold and windy days of winter. Now, no more spinning, no more mules. Cashmere and Fiat.

Easter

Our home tradition for Easter is full of lamb, both the roasted lamb that is the center-piece of Easter dinner and the flocks of marzipan lambs. They come in all sizes and are decorated with flags of peace and silver confetti and all different kinds of fancy and funny things like tiny feathers or roses made out of pink wafers. My mother likes to give them to visitors and relatives (we have a very large family) as Easter presents.

We still make our own *Pasta Reale* at Regaleali. You can buy almond flour and even ready-made marzipan in Sicily, but people who are attached to the old traditions make theirs from scratch. My friend Francesca di Carpinello, a painter who has given exposi-tions all over the world, is one of those. Sometimes she brings some of her marzipan and demonstrates *Cassata* for my cooking students. She also gives each of them one of her paintings to take home as a memento.

When Americans come for the cooking classes, one of the first things my mother does is ask them to make brownies for her. She really has a passion for chocolate. At Easter, she gathers all the little children she can for an Easter-egg hunt. She has enormous fun hiding chocolate eggs behind every bush in the garden and then helping the children find them.

OVERLEAF: *Almond blossoms decorate a Cassata (page 88), made with almond marzipan and candied fruits from last year's harvest.*

CASSATA *Cassata*

Pan di Spagna

6 eggs, at room temperature

2/3 cup sugar

1 teaspoon grated orange or lemon peel

1 cup flour, sifted

↶

Pasta Reale (page 148), preferably tinted green

Sciroppo di Zucchero

3/4 cup warm water

5 tablespoons sugar

2 tablespoons Grand Marnier

↶

3 cups Crema di Ricotta (page 63)

Glassa

1 1/2 cups confectioners' sugar

Juice of 1/2 lemon

1/2 teaspoon lemon extract

↶

Candied fruit, for garnish

Preheat the oven to 350°F. Butter and flour a 9-inch springform pan.

For the Pan di Spagna, put the eggs into a mixer bowl and beat for 5 minutes. Add the sugar and grated peel and continue to beat until ribbons form, about 15 minutes. Gradually fold in the flour. Pour into the springform pan and bake for 25 to 30 minutes, or until a needle inserted into the center of the cake comes out clean. Cool on a cake rack. Set it aside.

Cut the Pasta Reale log lengthwise into 1/2-inch-thick slices. Roll out 3 of the slices into strips about 1/8 to 1/4 inch thick. Knead the remaining Pasta Reale into a ball, wrap it in plastic, and store it in the refrigerator to use for another purpose. Line a 9-inch cassata pan, or a 9-inch pie pan with sloping sides, with plastic wrap. Line the sides of the pan with the Pasta Reale strips, slightly overlapping the ends. Press against the pan to form a smooth layer.

Make the sciroppo. Pour the water into a small bowl; add the sugar and the Grand Marnier. Stir to dissolve the sugar.

Cut the cake from top to bottom into 1/2-inch-thick slices and trim the crusts. Put a layer of slices on the bottom of the pan. Spoon 4 to 5 tablespoons of syrup on top.

Spread evenly with the crema. Carefully place another layer of cake slices on top. Add the rest of the syrup. Wrap the Cassata in plastic wrap and refrigerate for at least 1 hour.

Remove the outer plastic wrap from the Cassata and invert it onto a serving plate. Carefully lift off the pan and peel off the remaining plastic. Set the Cassata aside while you make the glassa.

Sift half of the confectioners' sugar into a bowl. Add half of the lemon juice and all of the lemon extract. Stir the liquid into the sugar, breaking up any lumps. Sift the remaining sugar into the bowl and add the rest of the lemon juice. Thin the icing with a little water, if necessary, until it has a thin spreading consistency and forms a smooth, shiny icing.

Ice the top of the Cassata, leaving the marzipan sides of the cake visible. If you are not using tinted marzipan, ice the entire cake. Decorate with whole and partially cut candied fruit. Refrigerate and allow to set for at least 1 to 2 hours before serving. This serves 10 to 12.

L'Estate

SUMMER

Summer in Sicily

is long and very hot. The earth and grass

are sunbaked and golden; there is straw everywhere.

At the height of the season, in mid-August, the

straw is burned to prepare the fields for sowing,

and the colors of the landscape change from yellow

to dark brown to black, and to green

when there has been rain.

BURNING THE FIELDS IS an ancient tradition, and sometimes when the men are not careful setting the straw on fire, it runs away and causes a lot of damage. Once the fire burns down, the tractors go out to plow the fields, digging deep and turning over the earth. The rich black soil, which Carmelo Di Martino, the caretaker of Case Vecchie, calls *la mamma di Regaleali*, comes up to the surface in big lumps. It smells good and fresh and brings some humidity to the air, which feels refreshing, since everything is so dry.

At about this time, we start looking up at the sky, hoping to see the black clouds that bring rain. The weather should break now, but often the sky is blue day after day.

Blue is the special color of Regaleali. The doors and windows are painted deep blue and the arches above them sky blue, the same shade as the tiled walls of the sheepfold and dairy. When my father was a young man, he and my grandfather traveled together to Tunisia. They brought back a taste for the way of using color they saw there.

Arriving at Regaleali, visitors sometimes remark, is like coming to an oasis. The hillsides are green and lush with vines, in contrast to the golden wheat fields and dark patches of fallow and scorched earth of the rest of central Sicily.

Almost all our vineyards are planted on slopes facing south, yet each has its own look and feel. Most were planned by Vincenzo Curcio, who knows which way the sun shines and which way the rain falls on every foot of the land. It's a good thing, too: the government limits how many acres can be planted with vines, so we can't afford to waste a single inch.

Each of our vineyards has a name. The practical reason is to help keep track of where the grapes have come from so that we know what went into each wine. My father enjoyed using our names, with "Saint" in front, for the vineyards. Vigneto di San Francesco is for my mother (Franca), San Lucio for my brother, Sant'Anna for me, and so on. During the harvest, Lucio and I compete to see whose vineyard produces the best and the most grapes. Sometimes I win, and sometimes he does. When that happens, I say there's been cheating, but it's only a joke.

Most of the grapes we grow are long-known varieties, such as the white Inzolia and Cataratto and the red Perricone, Nero d'Avola, and Nerello Mascalese. In addition, we have the unique Sauvignon Tasca, which is similar to the French Sauvignon Blanc, with the same leaf and structure but a somewhat different taste.

Our Sauvignon was discovered by a tenant farmer working the land in the 1940s. It created a small problem because we kept calling it Sauvignon and the experts said it wasn't quite that. My father organized a meeting of connoisseurs. Some said it was Sauvignon Blanc; some said it was not; still others said it was a modified clone, similar to the Sauvignon but not exactly the same. It was decided to call it Sauvignon but give it the family name, Tasca. This is the grape that gives our Regaleali Bianco and Nozze d'Oro wines their characteristic flavor.

Besides the indigenous varieties, we now grow many other grapes, including Pinot Noir, Chardonnay, and Cabernet Sauvignon, and there are ongoing experiments with new clones. The Pinot Noir and Chardonnay are used in our sparkling wines. We have a Crémant and a Brut, both called Conti d'Almerita after my father's title. Both are made by the *méthode champenoise*, the traditional French way, with fermentation in the bottle. Regaleali was the first—and, for a long time, the only—winery in Sicily to use this method. The Cabernet Sauvignon and the Chardonnay are used to make the wines bearing those names.

‖ The Feast of Sant'Anna ‖

In the traditional agricultural cycle, the fields are burned after the wheat harvest. Wheat has played a central role in the economy, history, and lore of Sicily for centuries. In my grandfather's day, Regaleali and all of Sicily lived on wheat. Though less significant now than in the past, wheat is still grown, and the harvest still is an important event. I am told that years ago it was quite a spectacle to see the reapers cutting the wheat by hand and threshing it. Now the work is done by machine—far less picturesque but more efficient.

The feast of Sant'Anna, my name day, falls on July 26. When I was a little girl, the saints were honored much more than they are today, and Sant'Anna, the mother of Mary, was very important. Since the feast day occurred toward the end of the harvest,

OVERLEAF: *Doors and windows at Case Grandi are painted "Regaleali blue."*

there was usually a big celebration. One year we even had fireworks. I scarcely remember those days, and now all we do is have a nice dinner party with a special menu of all the things I particularly like, including *Gelo di Melone*, a kind of pudding made with watermelon juice. It has a distinctly Arabian flavor. Susan Derecskey, who helped me write this book and who came truly to appreciate Sicilian food, says it reminds her of Turkish delight.

GELO DI MELONE *Watermelon Pudding*

One 6-pound watermelon
3/4 cup sugar
2/3 cup cornstarch
Jasmine flowers, candied fruit, or chopped unsalted pistachios,
    for garnish

Cut the watermelon in half and scoop out the pulp with a spoon, removing as many seeds as possible in the process. Put the pulp through a food mill or beat it with a mixer, using the paddle attachment. Drain the pureed flesh through a colander into a bowl, pushing the pulp against the sides of the colander to extract as much juice as possible. Measure out 4 1/2 cups of juice and discard the pulp.

Put the watermelon juice and the sugar in a saucepan, over medium heat. Use a strainer to sift in the cornstarch, whisking to blend. Cook over medium heat, using a wooden spoon or flexible spatula to stir and scrape the sides and bottom of the pot. Cook, stirring, for about 2 minutes after it boils. Pour into a 5-cup serving bowl and let it cool. Refrigerate the gelo until set, about 3 hours, or overnight. Just before serving, decorate the pudding with jasmine flowers, candied fruit, or chopped unsalted pistachios; it serves 8.

The other dessert we are likely to have on my name day is *Pignoccata*. Our old *monzù* Giovannino used to make it for me when I was a little girl, and I would pick off the balls of fried dough and eat them with my fingers.

PIGNOCCATA *Honeyed Pinecone Pastry*

1 orange
1¹/₂ cups flour
2 eggs, at room temperature
Pinch of salt
Oil, for frying
¹/₂ cup sugar
¹/₂ cup honey

Peel the orange in one long piece, and cut the peel into julienne strips about 5 inches long. Set aside for garnish. Squeeze the orange and reserve 3 tablespoons of the juice.

Mix together the flour, eggs, and salt. Knead about 2 to 3 minutes by hand or 1 minute in a food processor, until the dough is smooth. Cover the dough with plastic wrap and set it aside to rest for about 30 minutes.

Lightly roll out the dough 1 inch thick. Be careful not to squeeze out the air by flattening the dough, or it will not double in size when fried. Cut the dough into 1-inch strips, cut these strips crosswise into ¹/₂-inch strips, and then cut pea-sized pieces of dough.

Heat 2 inches of oil to about 375°F. in a deep saucepan. Fry the pieces of dough in batches. They will double in size, so do not crowd the pan. When golden, remove and drain on brown paper.

Combine the sugar, honey, and the reserved orange juice in a medium saucepan and cook over low heat, without stirring, until the honey and sugar melt and liquefy. Shake the pan from time to time. Add the pastry balls and use 2 large wooden spoons to gently mix and coat.

Transfer the pastry balls onto an oiled dish or a tray lined with parchment paper. Break the pastry into pieces before it cools completely and pile the pieces in the shape of a cone on a serving dish. Garnish with the strips of orange peel. Serve with coffee. This serves 6.

Starlike jasmine flowers add their heady aroma to Gelo di Melone (page 96).

We use our own honey to make this sticky Pignoccata (page 97).

Melons

Watermelons coincide with the hot sun of summer, and as long as it lasts, they are good. They appear in all sizes and shapes, either solid green or striped. The vendors pile them up for sale on street corners. They always keep some cold, so that when you stop to buy a melon to take home, you also buy a slice or two to eat right there on the spot—this is considered street food—but when we eat watermelon at home at the end of the meal, we eat slices with a knife and fork.

Besides watermelon we have two other melons, one with green skin, the other with yellow; both are called *melone d'inverno* (winter melon), and both have flesh that is white and very fragrant. Although they ripen at the end of summer and you can eat the yellow one already in September, we call them winter melon because they can be stored, hanging in a net bag, until December. These melons are grown commercially in western Sicily and kept in warehouses until Christmastime, when they are sold for a king's ransom. Fortunately, we grow and store our own. The melon is served chilled, usually with nothing on it. If a melon doesn't have much flavor, we sprinkle it with sugar and a few drops of lemon juice.

Orchard Fruits

There are many fruit trees at Regaleali, but often the worms and the birds get to them before we do. First to mature are the sour cherries, which we have in abundance and which we all like very much. Then come apricots, peaches (white and yellow), nectarines, and plums, both prunes and small golden plums like mirabelles.

Their beauty is short-lived in the withering heat, however, so after eating the fruit fresh for a while, we poach it and preserve it. Since the fruit ripens all at once, it's a race to gather and preserve as much as possible. All kinds of fruit are transformed into syrups, jams, and candied fruits. Whole fruit is put up in jars as in the past; now some fruit is frozen as well. The first-floor landing at the big house at Regaleali is lined with restaurant-sized freezers stocked with a year's supply of everything that is grown or raised on the land.

Later in the year, the fruits preserved in summer are used in fruit salads and desserts. The intense flavor of preserved fruit is much more satisfying than that of out-of-season fresh fruit picked thousands of miles away.

In winter, for example, my mother often serves sour-cherry syrup with ricotta cheese. In summer, we put the syrup in water with ice to drink against thirst; strawberry syrup is also refreshing used this way. Fruit syrup in water is a nice change from cold tea.

Mulberries

Another plentiful fruit is black mulberry. It stains your hands and clothes forever, but it does make a wonderful jam. I make my *Marmellata di Gelsi Neri* (Black Mulberry Jam) the same way I make all my jams and marmalades—equal amounts, by weight, of fruit and sugar boiled together with pectin. For the mulberry jam, I pass the mashed fruit through a sieve to remove some of the seeds. Years ago, it took huge amounts of sugar for the jams to keep, and we cooked them for hours on end, stirring and stirring and stirring. Now that commercial pectin is available, we use that; the preserves require less sugar and they set quickly, so the taste of the fruit remains intact.

A favorite dessert we use fruit preserves for is *Crostata*. The dough for this is *pasta frolla* (short pastry). Use whatever jam you have on hand.

CROSTATA *Jam Tart*

Pasta Frolla

> 2 *cups flour*
> ¼ *cup sugar*
> *Pinch of salt*
> 8 *tablespoons butter, cold, cut into* ½*-inch dice*
> 3 *egg yolks*
> ✧
> 2 *cups jam*

To make the pasta frolla, pour 1¾ cups of the flour out onto a work surface or into a bowl, make a well, and add the sugar and salt. Work the butter into the flour with your fingertips until the mixture has the consistency of cornmeal. Add the egg yolks, mixing them into the dough with your hands. Add additional flour as needed, but avoid overworking the dough. Form it into a disk, wrap it in plastic, and refrigerate it for at least 20 minutes.

Preheat the oven to 375°F. Line an 8-inch tart pan with parchment paper or aluminum foil.

Roll three-fourths of the dough into an 11- or 12-inch circle. Place it in the tart pan, shaping it to fit. Spread the jam in the shell. Roll out the remaining dough into a rectangle and cut ½-inch strips. Arrange the strips of dough in a lattice pattern on top of the jam. Bake for 30 to 40 minutes, until the pastry is a light golden color. Let this cool thoroughly. Serve at room temperature. This is very sweet, so give small servings, about 8.

Green Beans

Summer wouldn't be summer in Sicily without zucchini, eggplant, and tomatoes, the vegetable trio we practically live on during the hot months. But we also plant green beans in the garden to eat them all summer long, as a first course, boiled and buttered and served with triangles of fried bread arranged around the dish. Parboiled, breaded, and fried, they can be a first course or part of a *Fritto Misto*. Sometimes we have *Insalata di Fagiolini* (Green Bean Salad). For this, cooked green beans, alone or with tomatoes, are dressed with olive oil and vinegar, dried oregano, salt, and pepper; you serve this salad like any other in Italy, after the meat or fish.

Cucumbers

Cucumbers are another favorite. The Sicilian cucumber is long and thin and twisted, with dark-green, hairy skin; it is not too seedy. When the men are working in the fields, they eat cucumber against thirst. They peel it, cut a chunk as big as their mouth, and pop it in. It is very refreshing, especially after a midmorning snack of bread and cheese.

At the table, we often have a cooling dish of *Insalata di Cetrioli* (Cucumber Salad). Peel the cucumbers—partially or entirely, as you wish—and slice them thin; then dress them with oil and vinegar and season with pepper, salt, and a sprinkling of finely chopped parsley.

Peppers

Peppers—green, yellow, and red; big and small; hot and sweet—lend heat and color to Sicilian cuisine. We always keep some *Peperoni Arrostiti* (Roasted Sweet Peppers in Olive Oil) on hand in summer. We roast some brightly colored peppers, peel them, and remove the ribs and seeds. The peppers are sprinkled with salt and covered with oil. If you make a lot, they will keep for a week. Roasted peppers are perfect as part of a casual lunch when you are eating out of the garden.

Peperoni Ripieni (Stuffed Peppers) are light but filling. Usually when we make them, we just pick whatever is ripe at the moment, but it's nice when you can find different-colored peppers to brighten up the platter. The stuffing is basically the same as for *Sarde a Beccafico* (page 141), but we add some olives and capers to it. You can use the same stuffing for tomatoes and zucchini. The peppers need to be baked in a 300°F. oven for about forty minutes; tomatoes and zucchini a little less.

'We eat sweet peppers from the garden all summer long.

Hot peppers, whether round or long and twisted like the horns that bring good luck, are all called *peperoncini*. At Regaleali—and anywhere you go in Sicily—you will always find a shaker of *peperoncino in polvere* (ground hot pepper) and often a bottle of *olio al peperoncino* (hot pepper–flavored oil) on the table for those who want to add a little more heat to a dish. This also spares people who are sensitive to hot peppers from burning their lips on the hot peppers in a dish.

When the *peperoncini* are fresh, we put them in salads, not chopped but cut into small pieces, so that people who don't like them all that much can find the pieces and push them to one side of the plate. Still, putting the hot pepper in the dressing adds zest, especially to a salad like *Insalata di Mare*. For an everyday kind of meal, we make this fish salad with squid, cuttlefish, mussels, and octopus, sometimes with octopus alone. Pieces of leftover cooked fish are often added. Since cuttlefish and octopus can be difficult to find outside Sicily, I have used more squid than usual in this recipe.

INSALATA DI MARE *Seafood Salad*

1 to 1 1/2 pounds fresh squid, cleaned and cut into 1/2-inch pieces

1 pound small shrimp, shelled and cleaned

3 pounds mussels, bearded and scrubbed

2 cups cut-up leftover cooked fish

Salt

1 small hot pepper, cut into 1/4-inch pieces

Juice of 2 lemons

1/3 to 1/2 cup olive oil

1 small red onion, thinly sliced

1/4 cup chopped parsley

Cook the squid in boiling salted water for 5 to 7 minutes, until tender. Drain and set aside. Cook the shrimp in boiling salted water for about 2 minutes, until pink. Put the mussels in a medium sauté pan, cover, and cook over high heat for 3 to 5 minutes, shaking the pan once or twice. If the mussels have opened, they are done. If not, cover the pan and cook 1 to 2 minutes longer, until they are opened. Discard any that remain closed. Drain and remove the mussels from their shells.

Put the squid, shrimp, mussels, and leftover fish in a large serving bowl. Season with salt and the hot pepper to taste. Add the lemon juice, olive oil, onion, and chopped parsley. Toss to combine. This serves 8.

The best dish of all using hot peppers, though, is *Spaghetti Aglio, Olio, e Peperoncino* (Spaghetti with Garlic, Oil, and Hot Pepper), probably the most famous—and easiest—dish of the Kingdom of the Two Sicilies. I'm sorry, but I can't give a recipe. Only a Sicilian (or a Neapolitan) can make it right. The sauce, if you can even call it that, is just minced garlic heated in olive oil with chopped hot pepper. You have to feel the proportions in your heart.

Then there is the matter of the pasta. Sicilians are very particular about their pasta. For a long time it was the only food they could afford, and it is still the food they prefer. We in the south like our pasta far more al dente than they do in northern Italy. When I cook pasta for my son-in-law, Luca, who comes from the north, I have to remember to cook it longer than I normally would or he will look at me with big starving eyes. He doesn't say anything, but I know he is thinking, Why is your pasta always raw?

With spaghetti especially, the challenge for a Sicilian is to cook it to that point where it is perfect and get the pasta from the pot to the table in seconds. If you don't, you won't have my appreciation or that of any other Sicilian sitting at your table.

Tomatoes

We grow different kinds of tomatoes for different purposes, meaty San Marzano and Roma plum tomatoes for preserving and small round tomatoes and big beefsteak tomatoes for salad and stuffing. *Pomodori Ripieni* (Stuffed Tomatoes), made with small tomatoes, are usually filled with the typical Sicilian stuffing of breadcrumbs, pine nuts, and currants (page 141). Then they are drizzled with olive oil and baked. Beefsteak tomatoes are prepared the central Italian way as *Pomodori col Riso* (Tomatoes with Rice)—filled with a mixture of the pulp, rice, onion, and garlic and baked on a bed of sliced potatoes.

Cherry tomatoes are fairly new to Regaleali, but we all like them, either raw or cooked just until they burst, as in *Pasta con il Pomodoro Scoppiato*, a pasta dish my sister Costanza introduced the family to.

At the end of summer we pick cherry tomatoes and hang them until we want to eat them; we dry halved plum tomatoes on old screen doors. Red chili peppers—fresh in summer, dried in winter—add piquance to many dishes. Our green bell peppers are big and sweet.

PASTA CON IL POMODORO SCOPPIATO
Pasta with Burst Cherry Tomatoes

1 to 1¹/₂ pints cherry tomatoes (1 to 1¹/₂ pounds)
¹/₂ cup olive oil
2 garlic cloves, chopped
1 to 2 teaspoons dried oregano
Salt
Ground hot pepper
1 pound spaghetti
¹/₄ cup grated pecorino or parmesan (optional)

Cook the tomatoes in a large sauté pan in the olive oil with the garlic until they begin to burst and release their juices. Do this over medium heat so as not to burn the garlic before the tomatoes begin to release their juices. Once the tomatoes burst, raise the heat to evaporate the juices and thicken the sauce. Add the oregano. Season to taste with salt and ground hot pepper.

Cook the spaghetti in boiling salted water until al dente. Drain and pour into a serving bowl. Add half the sauce and toss well to mix. Put the remaining sauce on top. Serve immediately, and pass the grated cheese, if desired. This is enough for 4 as a first course.

Cherry-tomato plants are very prolific, so first we eat all we want, then when we get tired of them, we pick them and hang them in clusters. Certain fruits—winter melons and grapes, for example—are often hung this way. Since they don't touch any other surface, they keep very well. The cherry tomatoes picked at the end of summer last until the beginning of winter.

Another good tomato-and-pasta dish for summer is *Pasta con il Pomodoro Crudo*. The sauce is raw. If you have any left over, you can put it on *bruschetta* (grilled bread).

PASTA CON IL POMODORO CRUDO
Pasta with Fresh Tomato Sauce

2 pounds ripe tomatoes, peeled, seeded, and roughly chopped

1 teaspoon salt

1 tablespoon sugar

2 garlic cloves, minced

1/2 cup basil leaves

8 anchovy fillets, coarsely chopped

Ground hot pepper

1/2 cup olive oil

1 pound spaghetti

Put the tomatoes in a large colander set over a bowl and sprinkle with the salt, sugar, garlic, basil, anchovies, and ground hot pepper. Let the mixture stand for at least 1 hour. Transfer all to a serving bowl and add the olive oil. Set aside.

Bring a pot of salted water to a boil and add the spaghetti. Cook until al dente. Drain and place in the serving bowl. Toss with the sauce. Serve this immediately; it is enough for 4 as a first course.

A very quick cooked tomato sauce, really delicious when made with fresh tomatoes, is *Salsa Pic-Pac.* (You can also make it in winter with canned plum tomatoes.) Most people call this sauce *picchi-pacchi,* but Mario thinks *pic-pac* has a French—and therefore more elegant—ring. My father agrees. *Pic-pac* it is.

Salsiccia alla Griglia (opposite).

SALSA PIC-PAC *Chunky Tomato Sauce*

1 large red onion, coarsely chopped

2 garlic cloves, minced

¹/₄ cup olive oil

2 pounds ripe tomatoes, peeled and coarsely chopped

¹/₂ cup basil leaves, torn

1 teaspoon sugar

Salt

Black pepper

Sauté the onion and garlic in the olive oil in a saucepan for 2 to 3 minutes, until slightly golden. Add the tomatoes and cook, stirring, for 2 to 3 minutes. Reduce the heat and add half the basil, the sugar, and salt and pepper to taste. Partially cover the pan and continue to cook 10 to 15 minutes, stirring occasionally, until the sauce thickens. The time it takes the sauce to thicken will depend upon the variety and ripeness of your tomatoes. Taste and adjust the seasonings. Add the remaining basil. This makes about 3¹/₂ cups of sauce.

While there are still plenty of fresh tomatoes, we make a chicken dish with them, *Galletto al Pomodoro.* The tomatoes cook down to a thick sauce that has all the flavor of summer in it. As with the *pic-pac,* you can use canned tomatoes in winter, but the sauce won't be quite as satisfying.

GALLETTO AL POMODORO *Chicken with Tomatoes*

One 2- to 3-pound chicken, quartered

3 to 4 tablespoons olive oil

1 stalk celery, blanched and chopped

1 large onion, chopped

2 pounds tomatoes, peeled, seeded, and chopped

1 teaspoon sugar

Salt

Black pepper

Remove and discard the chicken wing tips, backbone, breastbone, and ribs.

Pour the oil into a 10- or 12-inch skillet and sauté the chicken until golden brown. Remove the chicken from the pan and pour off the excess fat. Deglaze the pan with ¼ cup of water, scraping up any bits stuck to the bottom.

Return the chicken to the pan and add the celery, onion, tomatoes, sugar, and salt and pepper to taste. Simmer, covered, for about 30 to 40 minutes, until the chicken is tender. Remove the chicken from the pan. Put it on a serving dish and keep it warm. Taste the sauce and adjust the seasonings. Pour the sauce over the chicken and serve warm. This serves 4 as a main course.

The oldest and most traditional way of eating fresh tomatoes—and the best way when they are just picked out of your garden—is simply sprinkled with salt. This is called *Pomodoro a Strica-Sale* (Tomato Rubbed with Salt). Sometimes we make a little "salad" on the plate by drizzling them with olive oil as well.

When I used to stay with my grandfather at Regaleali, his maid Lorita would sometimes bring some of her tomato salad to share with me for breakfast in bed. I loved it and considered it a great treat. Now when I make my own tomato salad, I often add other ingredients, like arugula or purslane. But not for breakfast.

Tomato salad is usually dressed with oil and vinegar, dried oregano, salt, and pepper. I usually put in a few thin slices of red onion, but only if I have good ones, fresh and not too strong. I also like to add bits of fresh lemon. This salad, *Insalata di Pomodoro e Cipolla* (Tomato and Onion Salad), is a classic. You'll want to serve any tomato salad with some good bread for dipping.

We often serve this tomato salad together with *Insalata di Patate e Capperi* in summer. They are very good with *Salsiccia alla Griglia* (Grilled Sausage). The sausage, which is flavored with fennel seeds, is coiled tight with fresh bay leaves and slices of red onion stuck in between; then it is grilled over the coals.

INSALATA DI PATATE E CAPPERI *Potato Salad with Capers*

2 pounds waxy potatoes, scrubbed
¼ cup capers, rinsed
1 tablespoon dried oregano
1 medium red onion, cut into thin wedges
3 tablespoons red wine vinegar
½ cup olive oil
Salt
Black pepper

Cook the potatoes in boiling salted water for about 40 minutes, or until done. Avoid overcooking.

Peel and cut the potatoes into bite-sized pieces. Put them in a bowl and add the capers, oregano, and onion. Dress with vinegar and oil. Season with salt and pepper to taste. Serve cold or at room temperature. This serves 4 to 6 as a side dish.

There are so many tomatoes, the whole month of August is dedicated to preserving them. All the women make their own tomato sauce. Sicilians practically live on spaghetti and tomato sauce; they eat it every day of their life. If you offer them something different, they eat it to please you, all the while longing to get back to their spaghetti.

At Regaleali, we mostly make the smooth tomato sauce, *Salsa di Pomodoro Passata*, or simply *la salsa*. We use it all year long as the basis for other, more complicated sauces. We bottle it in old wine bottles, which visitors sometimes find amusing. Depending on the size of the family, people put up their *salsa* in different-sized bottles—wine bottles, half-liter beer bottles for people who live alone, or mineral-water bottles three times that size for big families. (More and more in Sicily we have to buy bottled water because the tap water has become undrinkable.)

Estratto di Pomodoro (page 115), molded into the traditional pinecone shape, with fresh bay leaves.

SALSA DI POMODORO PASSATA *Smooth Tomato Sauce*

2 pounds ripe tomatoes
1 large onion, finely chopped
2 garlic cloves, minced
¹⁄₄ cup olive oil
1 teaspoon sugar
¹⁄₄ cup basil leaves
Salt
Black pepper

If using plum tomatoes, cut them in half lengthwise. If the tomatoes are large, cut them into quarters. Put the tomatoes into a medium, nonreactive saucepan. Cover and cook for 15 to 25 minutes, until soft. The length of time the tomatoes take to cook will depend upon their variety and ripeness. Once they are soft, pass the tomatoes through a food mill and reserve the puree in a bowl.

Sauté the onion and garlic in the olive oil for about 2 to 3 minutes, until golden. Add the tomato puree, the sugar, basil, and salt and pepper to taste. Cook for at least 20 minutes, until the sauce is reduced and thickened to your liking. This makes 2¹⁄₂ to 3 cups of salsa.

Besides making the ubiquitous *salsa,* we can whole tomatoes and chopped tomatoes. Tomatoes are also put out to dry in the sun. Plum tomatoes are cut in half lengthwise, spread out on screens, and sprinkled with salt. It takes about a week for them to dry thoroughly. Then they are brought in.

I pack these *Pomodori Seccati al Sole* (Sun-dried Tomatoes) in oil. I take two halves and make a "sandwich" with chopped garlic, fresh basil, dried oregano, and a piece of fresh hot red pepper in the middle and put it in a jar. When the jar is almost full, I pour in some olive oil, push the tomatoes down with two fingers to make sure there is no air between the layers, and fill the jar with enough olive oil to cover the top layer of tomatoes. They need to be stored for about a month before you eat them. We serve these tomatoes as part of the antipasto course, along with cubes of *primo sale* (young pecorino), olives, and homemade preserved eggplant or mushrooms, or as part of an informal lunch.

ESTRATTO DI POMODORO

The biggest preserving job of all is to make *Estratto di Pomodoro* (Sun-dried Tomato Extract), which we use in *ragù*. This is done by putting tomato sauce out to dry in the sun. After a few days, it hardens into a dark extract that is far denser and richer than ordinary tomato paste. Making *estratto* has unfortunately come to be regarded as too much work, and it is done less and less often in Sicily. Because of my interest in reviving old culinary traditions, however, a couple of years ago we started to make *estratto* for ourselves at Regaleali.

Then one day I decided to try to make *Estratto di Pomodoro* on a grand scale to sell along with my other preserves. I knew from the beginning I would have to be very stubborn because when you want to do something in Sicily, everyone tries to discourage you at first. But then, little by little, they come around and start being helpful—though always with an air of disbelief.

When I started asking people about *estratto*, I got all different opinions on what kind of tomato is best—round or pointed—but everyone agreed that the tomatoes have to be ripe and that *estratto* takes a huge amount of tomatoes. They also agreed that I would need the help of God to keep the sun shining and, perhaps, send a breeze to speed the drying.

The first time I made *estratto* on a grand scale, I had five assistants, all hardworking people. We filled a giant caldron twice a day with more than two hundred pounds of tomatoes at a time.

All that fruit had to be washed and the juice and seeds squeezed out. The authentic way is to stick your thumb into the side of a tomato, tear it open, and squeeze it, but I used a knife to spare my finger. We put the smashed fruit in slotted plastic baskets to drain, pressing down with our hands to get out more juice. When we had filled several baskets, we dumped them into the caldron, and Carmelo lit the fire underneath. His job was not an enviable one. He had to stand by the fire and stir constantly to prevent even one tomato from sticking to the bottom and burning. Little by little, as the first tomatoes shrank from the heat, he put in all the rest we had prepared. This took about an hour.

Suddenly we could hear Carmelo shout from the fire room, "*Che ora è?*" ("What's the time?") and that made us all happy, for we knew this meant "*La peniola bolle*" ("The caldron is boiling"). Our two hundred pounds of tomatoes and three pounds of salt had to cook for one hour. At this stage, the important thing is to keep the fire under control so that the sauce doesn't boil over. After an hour, we transferred the hot sauce to large basins to stand overnight and we covered the basins with screens to keep the flies from falling in.

Early each morning we started the day by passing the cooked tomatoes through an

OVERLEAF: *Tomato sauce for Estratto di Pomodoro dries under the Sicilian sun.*

electric food mill. Then I would take a jug of the sauce and pour it onto one of the twelve wooden tables that had been set up in the courtyard of Case Vecchie. As with the selection of the tomatoes, the question of what kind of tables to use provoked some spirited discussion, specifically, whether or not they should be tilted to let the liquid run off. Maria Tartaglia—whom we call Maria, the Mother of Twins, to distinguish her from all the other Marias, it being a very common name here—and I finally decided we wouldn't listen to any more advice and tilted the tables. No *estratto* could be better than what Maria makes, so she had the last word.

When you are pouring the sauce, the trick is to pour just enough so it doesn't run off the table and to pour it fast, because the sooner it is poured and spread, the sooner it starts to dry. I started spreading out the sauce on the tables under the strong hot sun. All day long I kept going from table to table to spread the sauce, sometimes using my fingers, sometimes a spoon or a dough scraper, until the sun set. It seems I provided great entertainment for the farm workers who came by to watch me and offer their opinions, never saying what was really on their minds, of course—that I must be crazy to put myself through all this. Actually, there were moments when I thought they were right.

Once all the sauce had been spread and the food mill washed, we started on the next batch of tomatoes. By nightfall, the sauce on the tables had shrunk to a paste, and we gradually transferred it from twelve to two tables. For two more days we kept spreading the paste. When it was reduced to one small table, we brought it inside to let it dry some more. When the *estratto* was the consistency of modeling clay, we put it into ceramic containers. For another day, we kneaded and caressed it with our oiled hands. Then we covered the *estratto* with plastic wrap until we were ready to put it into jars and label them.

We went on like this for ten days. From more than four thousand pounds of tomatoes, we produced seven containers of *Estratto di Pomodoro*, thirty-four pounds each. At this moment it was no longer tomato extract; it was pure gold.

Eggplant

As with tomatoes, we grow several different varieties of eggplant. Some are large, some small, some oval, others round, and each has a different purpose. Besides the common purple eggplant, sometimes called a Turkish eggplant, we have a white-skinned eggplant and the Tunisina, which is round with striped violet-and-white skin. It is not bitter at all, so you don't have to salt it before cooking. You do have to salt the bitter Turkish eggplant, though, to draw off some of its juices. I salt the eggplant slices on just one side and stack them in a colander with a plate or pot lid on top, weighted down with a heavy stone or a large can.

The Tunisina is particularly good for *Melanzane a Cotoletta*, also called *Milanese dei Poveri* (Poor Man's Cutlet) because it looks like a breaded cutlet but isn't meat. The flesh of the Tunisina eggplant stays white, like chicken breast. Eggplant cutlets are usually served hot with potatoes and a salad.

MELANZANE A COTOLETTA *Breaded Eggplant Cutlets*

2 pounds eggplant, trimmed and peeled
Salt
1 cup flour
Black pepper
3 eggs, beaten
1 1/2 cups fine breadcrumbs
Oil, for frying

Cut the eggplants lengthwise into 3/4-inch slices, salt them, stack them in a colander, and weight them. Allow the eggplant to drain for at least 30 minutes, but preferably for 1 hour.

Put the flour into a shallow bowl and season it with salt and pepper. Put the eggs into another bowl and the breadcrumbs into a third. Dip each slice of eggplant first in the flour, then the eggs, and finally the breadcrumbs. Set aside in a single layer until all the slices are coated.

Heat 1 inch of oil in a deep sauté pan until it sizzles when you test it with the edge of a slice of eggplant. Fry the eggplant in batches without crowding the pan, drain on paper towels, and serve hot. This serves 8 to 10 as a side dish.

Roses grow in the courtyard at Case Grandi.

Plain fried eggplant slices—that is, not breaded—are often served with pasta, usually spaghetti, either plain or with tomato sauce and basil leaves, or instead of zucchini in *Pasta con le Zucchine Fritte*. When frying eggplant, always remember that it has a prodigious thirst for oil and can absorb enormous amounts of it, especially if the oil isn't hot enough.

Eggplant is also fried for *Melanzane a Quaglia* (Eggplant Quails), a Sicilian specialty. This is how the Sicilian food historian Denti del Pirajno describes it in his book *Siciliani a Tavola*: "You have to cut the eggplant like a flower and deep-fry it. And don't lack imagination and eat it only with spaghetti. A *quaglia* lives very well on its own, sprinkled with chopped parsley and garlic, or in the middle of a soft roll."

The way to cut the eggplant for this dish is to slice it from top to bottom, stopping about one inch from the base. As the eggplant fries, the slices curl back; when it is done, it looks like a flower or a quail's tail or an octopus, as you wish.

Because fried eggplant absorbs so much oil, many people prefer *Melanzane alla Griglia* (Grilled Eggplant). When eaten as a side dish, that is, not with spaghetti, grilled eggplant slices are usually dressed with olive oil, a drop of lemon juice or vinegar, and salt and pepper and seasoned with garlic and herbs; I find they are particularly good with mint.

Caponata di Melanzane, a tasty eggplant relish, is put up in large quantities every summer. The sweet-and-sour sauce gives it a very special flavor.

CAPONATA DI MELANZANE *Eggplant Caponata*

2 pounds eggplant, peeled and cut into 1-inch cubes

Salt

1 large onion, coarsely chopped

1/4 cup olive oil

1 cup Salsa di Pomodoro Passata (page 114)

1/2 cup tomato paste, thinned with 1/2 cup water

1 stalk celery, strings removed and coarsely chopped

6 ounces green olives, pitted and cut into thirds (3/4 to 1 cup)

4 tablespoons capers, rinsed and drained

3 tablespoons sugar

1/2 cup white wine vinegar

Black pepper

Oil, for frying

Hard-boiled eggs, cut in half, for garnish

Chopped parsley, for garnish

Put the eggplant cubes in a colander and salt them. Let them stand for 1 hour to drain while you make the sauce.

Sauté the onion in the olive oil for 2 to 3 minutes, until just golden. Add the salsa and thinned tomato paste. Simmer, uncovered, until thickened, 5 to 8 minutes. Add the celery, olives, capers, and sugar. Stir in the vinegar and salt and pepper to taste. Simmer for 15 to 20 minutes, then transfer the sauce to a large bowl and cool.

Heat 1 inch of oil in a large sauté pan. Wipe the eggplant pieces dry, and fry them, a batch at a time, until golden brown. Drain well on paper towels.

Add the eggplant to the sauce and mix well. Taste for seasoning, then let cool. Pile the caponata in a pyramid and surround it with hard-boiled eggs, sprinkle with chopped parsley, and serve at room temperature. This makes 6 cups of caponata, which will serve 8 as a side dish.

Melanzane Ripiene (Stuffed Eggplants) are often served at Regaleali. We fill the eggplants with caciocavallo cheese, garlic, and basil leaves and cook them in simmering tomato sauce. Sometimes we stuff eggplants (or zucchini) with leftover *ragoncino*. To do this, you cut small eggplants or zucchini in half lengthwise, hollow out the shells, and fill them with the *ragoncino* (page 134). Fry lightly, add a cup of water and half a beef bouillon cube, cover, and simmer until soft, about fifteen minutes.

Zucchini

Several kinds of Sicilian summer squash, which don't look or taste alike at all, are called *zucchine*. One of these is very similar in taste and texture to the common American zucchini that grows close to the ground, hiding under big green leaves.

When this plant is in bloom, we pick some of the flowers to make *Fiori di Zucca a Spezzatino* (Braised Zucchini Blossoms) for a first dish. You sauté some chopped onion in olive oil, then add the blossoms and a little wine and water. They take only a few minutes to cook.

Mario takes the flowers for *Fiori di Zucca Fritti* (Fried Zucchini Blossoms) to serve with drinks before dinner or to include in a *Fritto Misto*. He fills the flower with as much finely diced mozzarella as it can hold and a small piece of anchovy and folds it over. Then he dredges it in flour, dips it in egg wash, coats it with breadcrumbs, and fries it. These fried zucchini blossoms are also often served as an appetizer.

This kind of zucchini is best, though, in my mother's *Pasta con le Zucchine Fritte*. In the classic dish, spaghetti is topped with slices of fried zucchini in a little of the oil they were fried in. My mother's special touch is to make a sauce with butter, milk, and some of the pasta water; it makes the dish more mellow. Then she garnishes it with basil and grated parmesan.

PASTA CON LE ZUCCHINE FRITTE *Pasta with Fried Zucchini*

1 pound small zucchini
Salt
1 cup olive oil
1 pound spaghetti
2 tablespoons milk
1 tablespoon butter
Black pepper
Basil leaves, shredded, for garnish
1/4 cup grated parmesan, for garnish

Wash the zucchini well, scrubbing with a brush. Trim the ends of the zucchini and slice it 1/4 inch thick. Salt the slices, place them in a colander, weight them, and let them stand for 30 minutes to drain. Heat the olive oil in a sauté pan and fry the zucchini until deep brown on both sides. Remove and drain the zucchini on brown paper. Reserve 3 tablespoons of the oil for the sauce and reserve the rest for another purpose.

Cook the spaghetti in boiling salted water until al dente. Put the milk, butter, reserved oil, and salt and pepper to taste in a serving bowl. Stir in about 2 tablespoons of the pasta water. Drain the spaghetti and transfer to the bowl. Add half the zucchini and toss. Put the remaining zucchini on top. Garnish with basil leaves and parmesan, and serve hot. This serves 4 to 6 as a pasta course.

My mother makes the best pasta dishes in the world. Starting with nothing, she brings to the table something that will stay in your dreams forever. Even if Mario or Salvatore, who cooks when Mario is away, is around, my mother will be in the kitchen supervising the operation of draining and dressing the spaghetti. She's also tasting everything on the stove. None of us goes with her—we all feel sure that if she is there, every dish will be phenomenal.

My mother really enjoys eating and seeing other people eat. She is very proud that she remembers all the different dishes that each one of her guests prefers. She knows her power, and she loves it when someone sits at her table for the second time and says, "I remember the last time I was here and we had the most wonderful . . ."

Another kind of zucchini we have is called *zucca lunga.* This is the one we use most. It is a long, thin squash, with smooth, pale-green skin, and it tastes very bland. It grows so long that we usually build a trellis for the plant to climb on—sometimes you see it hanging from a tree—but even then the squash often touches the ground.

We cook zucchini flowers for an appetizer and fry the squash itself to serve with spaghetti (page 123). Zucca lunga is grown on a trellis; I turn these squash into a special marmelatta (page 143). Basil and bay flourish in every patch of sunshine.

One way we eat *zucca lunga* is boiled with its tender vines and leaves, which are called *tennerumi*. In fact, the name for the dish in dialect is *Tennerumi e Cucuzze* (Leaves and Squash). It does not look very attractive, but most Sicilians like it. They say it "cleans the stomach."

I like to make this more like a soup, *Minestra di Tennerumi e Cucuzze*. It is very special and probably can't be duplicated anywhere outside Sicily, but I'll give you a recipe anyway in case you want to try it with a large zucchini that you overlooked in the garden. I am told that you can safely eat the vines and leaves of American zucchini; if you are inclined to try, just cut off eighteen-inch lengths and chop them roughly. Otherwise, substitute spinach or chard leaves. When we make this soup, the weather is usually so hot we have to cool the soup down by setting the tureen in a basin of ice, which also stops the pasta from overcooking.

MINESTRA DI TENNERUMI E CUCUZZE *Zucchini Soup*

1 medium red onion, chopped

¹/₂ cup olive oil

1¹/₂ pounds zucchini, ends trimmed, cut into 1-inch chunks

2 cups tennerumi, roughly cut, or spinach or chard, stemmed and roughly cut

¹/₄ cup basil leaves, torn

3 small tomatoes, peeled, seeded, and chopped

Salt

Black pepper

6 cups water

1 beef bouillon cube

¹/₄ pound spaghetti, broken into 1-inch pieces

¹/₄ cup grated pecorino or parmesan, for garnish

Olive oil, for garnish

Sauté the onion in the olive oil in a saucepan for 2 to 3 minutes, until just golden. Add the zucchini and tennerumi and stir to blend. Stir in half the basil, the tomatoes, and salt and pepper to taste. Add enough of the 6 cups water to cover, reduce the heat, and cook, partly covered, for 15 minutes.

Add the rest of the water and the bouillon cube and bring the soup to a boil. Add the spaghetti and cook until al dente. Pour the soup into a tureen and set it in a cold-water bath to cool rapidly.

Sprinkle the remaining basil on top of the soup. Serve with the grated pecorino and oil for drizzling. This soup serves 6.

In the dish *Zucca Lunga a Spezzatino*, the zucchini gets a lift from basil. Our basil is very aromatic, and we frequently use the leaves, whole or shredded, to garnish a dish.

Zucca Lunga a Spezzatino *Zucchini with Tomatoes and Basil*

1 medium onion, chopped

1/2 cup olive oil

1 pound plum tomatoes, peeled and chopped

1 1/2 pounds zucchini, cut into 1-inch chunks

1 chicken bouillon cube

3/4 cup water

Salt

Black pepper

1/2 cup basil leaves, torn, for garnish

1/4 cup grated parmesan, for garnish

Sauté the onion in the olive oil in a saucepan for 2 to 3 minutes, until just golden. Add the tomatoes and cook for another 2 to 3 minutes. Add the zucchini and stir to mix. Add the bouillon cube, water, and salt and pepper to taste. Cover and cook for 15 to 20 minutes, until the zucchini is soft. Pour into a serving dish and sprinkle with torn basil leaves and parmesan. Serve at room temperature. It is enough for 6 as a side dish.

Herbs

Our basil makes a very aromatic pesto. In *Pasta con il Pesto al Pomodoro* there are two unusual twists—tomato is added to the pesto, and a thinly sliced potato is cooked together with the spaghetti. By the time the spaghetti is al dente, the potato has started to break up into little pieces. This recipe makes about three cups of pesto, so you will have some left over. Use the leftover pesto as a marinade for grilled fish or a topping on *bruschetta.*

The recipe calls for a food processor, but in the past a mortar and pestle would have been used. No cook could have been without them in the kitchen. That is still true, though more and more Italian housewives are getting food processors. I still have a few mortars of marble or stone decorating some corner or another of the house, but I have a food processor in my new kitchen at Regaleali.

PASTA CON IL PESTO AL POMODORO
Pasta with Tomato-Basil Pesto

3 cups basil leaves

1 cup parsley leaves

2 garlic cloves, peeled

1/3 cup grated pecorino

1/2 cup pine nuts

3 small tomatoes, peeled and seeded

1 1/2 cups olive oil

Salt

Black pepper

1 potato, peeled and thinly sliced

1 pound linguine

Put all the ingredients except the potato and the pasta into a food processor. Process until they form a rough paste.

Cook the potato and the pasta in boiling salted water until the pasta is al dente. Drain the pasta, then transfer it and the potato to a bowl, pour about 3/4 cup of the pesto over, and toss to coat. Put some of the remaining pesto on top, and serve hot. This serves 4 as a pasta course.

You will have about 1 1/2 cups of pesto left over. Put the leftover pesto in a glass jar, cover with olive oil, and refrigerate. It will keep for 4 to 5 days. If you freeze it, it will last forever.

Geraniums in a giara.

Mario doesn't use herbs as much as I do, but he wouldn't be without them either. I used to think his herb-and-caper sauce for baked swordfish could not be beat, but then one day my friend Faith Willinger was visiting from Florence, and she threw together her *Salmoriglio al Finocchietto* (Herb Sauce with Wild Fennel) for grilled bluefish. It was amazing. She started with a base of chopped herbs and capers and added some grated lemon peel, wild-fennel pollen, and fresh hot peppers for an entirely original sauce that was perfect with the grilled fish.

Another dish that takes a mixed-herb topping is *Minestrone Freddo*. This soup, which is served cold, has in it everything you can think of, starting with a base of onions, garlic, potatoes, carrots, celery, and tomatoes. Zucchini is usually added, as well as some tender zucchini leaves and blossoms. If there are green beans in the garden, they go in, too. Next, whatever greens and as much of them as can fit into the pot—escarole, chard, cabbage, and so on—a piece of pecorino or parmesan rind, and bouillon cubes and water. To keep the soup green, we start the cooking without the lid and put it on later, slightly askew. All summer long we have a container of this soup in the refrigerator with another container of cold cooked rice or pasta to stir in just before serving. The herb garnish is added at the last minute.

You can vary the herb topping, using whatever herbs you have on hand. On one occasion when I felt the soup really needed a boost, I chopped parsley, basil, and garlic together and mixed in some ground hot red pepper and grated pecorino cheese. It was pretty to look at and good to eat.

MINESTRONE FREDDO *Cold Minestrone*

2 large onions, sliced

4 garlic cloves, minced

2 stalks celery, chopped

2 carrots, chopped

1 pound waxy potatoes, peeled and cubed

4 tomatoes, peeled, seeded, and chopped

1 small zucchini, cut into ¹/₂-inch pieces

¹/₄ pound green beans, trimmed and cut into 2-inch lengths

10 cups stemmed and roughly chopped green, such as Swiss chard, escarole,
*   kale, cabbage*

2 chicken bouillon cubes

One 2-inch-square rind of pecorino or parmesan or 1 piece leftover ham or ham bone

2 cups cooked rice, cold

¹/₃ to ¹/₂ cup olive oil

¹/₂ cup grated pecorino or parmesan

¹/₂ cup chopped parsley, sage, fresh bay, rosemary, thyme, and basil leaves,
*   for garnish*

Salt

Black pepper

Grated pecorino or parmesan, for garnish

Put all the vegetables in a large pot, add the bouillon cubes and water to come halfway up the ingredients, and bring the soup to a boil, uncovered. Turn down the heat and add the cheese rind. Simmer, partially covered, for 1 hour. Cool the minestrone and refrigerate. Just before serving, add the rice, oil to taste, grated cheese, and chopped herbs. Season to taste with salt and pepper. Serve this cold or at room temperature, garnished with additional cheese. This serves 10 to 12 as a first course.

Fritto Misto

Fritto Misto (Mixed Fry) is one of the classic Sicilian "big" dishes. When Mario makes it, it nearly always includes *Melanzane a Cotoletta*, *Fiori di Zucca Fritti*, or certain other vegetables—onions, green beans, and cauliflower, depending on the season—that are dipped in batter and fried.

A full *Fritto Misto* would include *Arancine* or *Timbaletti*, one or the other. When you make the *Arancine*, be sure to plan ahead to prepare the *ragoncino* the day before. You will have quite a bit left over—it's hard to make a small quantity—so refrigerate it or freeze it to use later as a sauce for pasta or to stuff eggplant or zucchini. The rice balls can be rolled in flour, beaten eggs, and breadcrumbs, if you like, to form a stronger shell. *Arancine* and *Timbaletti* can also be served as a first course. Allow two per person.

Panelle are almost certain to be in the *Fritto Misto*. These little chick-pea chips are street food; you find them at every *friggitoria* (fry shop) in Palermo. There they are tucked into a soft roll while hot, to be eaten while you walk down the street or just stand around to watch the passing scene. Besides *Arancine*, *Panelle*, potato croquettes, fried cauliflower and cardoons, and so on, the *friggitorie* sell *Melanzane a Quaglia* nestled in soft rolls. Students love to eat this kind of food during recess.

Also part of the *Fritto Misto* are *Spiedini di Mozzarella e Acciughe* and *Uova alla Monacale*, both of which need a little bit of béchamel. For a full *Fritto Misto*, we would make a batch, take some for the *spiedini* and *uova*, then use the rest to make *Croquettes di Latte* (Béchamel Croquettes). The béchamel is formed into little sausage shapes, then breaded and fried.

For Arancine, Mario shapes a rice ball and fills it with ragoncino. He seals spiedini with a thick béchamel (pages

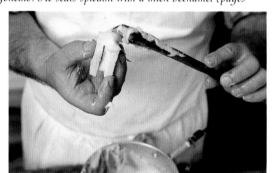

134 and 135). Fritto Misto, above and opposite, includes Fiori di Zucca Fritti and onions dipped in batter and fried.

ARANCINE *Stuffed Rice Balls*

Ragoncino

1 pound lean ground beef

¹/₃ cup olive oil

³/₄ cup mixed minced onion, celery, and carrot

Ground hot pepper

¹/₂ cup frozen peas

2 cups Salsa di Pomodoro Passata (page 114)

Risotto

3¹/₂ quarts water

4 beef bouillon cubes

Salt

4 tablespoons margarine

8 tablespoons butter

2 pounds Arborio rice

8 saffron threads or ¹/₂ teaspoon powdered saffron

¹/₂ cup grated parmesan

2 large eggs, lightly beaten

↪

1¹/₂ cups fine breadcrumbs

Oil, for frying

Start the ragoncino at least one day before you make the rice balls. Cook the ground beef in a dry sauté pan, stirring to break it up, until lightly browned. Drain off the fat.

Put the olive oil and the minced vegetables in a medium saucepan and sauté for 6 to 8 minutes, until soft and barely golden. Add hot pepper to taste. Add the cooked meat, peas, and salsa and simmer, covered, for 30 to 45 minutes, until the sauce thickens. Cool, cover, and refrigerate the ragoncino.

To make the risotto, bring the water to a boil, add the bouillon cubes and salt to taste, and continue boiling until the bouillon is dissolved. Melt the margarine and 2 tablespoons of the butter in a large saucepan and add the rice, stirring, until the grains are well coated. Stir in the bouillon by the ladleful, waiting until each is absorbed before adding the next. Add the saffron when the risotto has cooked for about 10 minutes. Continue to add the bouillon and stir until the risotto is smooth and creamy with an al dente consistency. There may be some bouillon left over, which you can refrigerate or freeze to use for another purpose. Add the remaining butter and the parmesan and stir to blend. Pour the rice into a large bowl and set it in a cold-water bath. Add the eggs as soon as the rice is no longer hot enough to cook them.

Make the rice balls while the risotto is still warm and malleable—it gets difficult to shape as it cools. Set out the cool ragoncino, which should be as dry as possible, and pour the breadcrumbs into a soup bowl. Wet your hands and shape some rice into a ball in a cupped hand, making an indentation in the center to form a well. Spoon about 1 tablespoon of ragoncino in the center of the well. Cover with additional rice and shape to form a ball about the size of a small tangerine, 2 to 2¹/₂ inches in diameter. Roll each ball in the breadcrumbs and set it aside until you have used up all the rice. Some ragoncino will be left over. Refrigerate or freeze it to use for another purpose.

Heat 2¹/₂ to 3 inches of oil in a deep fryer or a saucepan to about 325°F.

Fry the rice balls, turning them in the oil, until evenly cooked and crisp and deep golden on the outside, about 3 minutes. To test, insert a metal skewer and remove it. If the skewer feels warm to the touch, the rice ball is cooked. Drain on paper towels, and serve immediately. This makes about 24 Arancine, enough to serve 12 as a first course, more as part of a Fritto Misto.

SPIEDINI DI MOZZARELLA E ACCIUGHE
Mozzarella and Anchovy Tidbits

Béchamel
3 tablespoons butter
4 tablespoons flour
1 cup milk
Salt
Black pepper
↔
6 slices sandwich bread
6 anchovy fillets
3 to 4 ounces fresh mozzarella, sliced very thin
¹/₂ cup flour
Salt
Black pepper
1 egg, beaten with 1 teaspoon water
¹/₂ cup fine breadcrumbs
Oil, for frying

Melt the butter for the béchamel in a small saucepan and remove from the heat. Add the 4 tablespoons flour, whisking to incorporate thoroughly. Put the pan back on the heat and add the milk gradually, continuing to whisk to prevent lumps. Continue to whisk the béchamel as it thickens. It should be very dense. Season to taste with salt and pepper and set aside.

Trim the crusts off the bread and arrange the slices on the counter. Put 2 anchovy fillets on each of 3 slices of bread and cover with mozzarella, trimming to fit. Cover with the other slices of bread. Cut each sandwich into 4 squares and seal the edges with béchamel. You will have some béchamel left over. Refrigerate or freeze it for another use.

Put the 1/2 cup flour in a shallow bowl and season it with salt and pepper. Put the egg in another bowl and the breadcrumbs in a third. Dip each sandwich in flour, egg, and breadcrumbs. Set aside until all are done.

Pour enough oil into a deep fryer or a large sauté pan to float the sandwiches. Heat the oil until it sizzles when tested with the edge of one of the sandwiches. Fry the sandwiches in batches, turning them to brown evenly. Drain on paper towels and serve hot. This serves 6 as part of a Fritto Misto.

PANELLE *Chick-pea Chips*

3 1/4 cups water
1/2 pound chick-pea flour
2 teaspoons salt
Black pepper
Oil, for frying

Pour the water into a saucepan and add the chick-pea flour, whisking to prevent lumps. Season with the salt and add pepper to taste. Cook over medium heat, stirring constantly, until the mixture begins to thicken. Remove from the heat.

Working quickly with a flexible spatula, thinly spread the dough 1/8 to 1/4 inch thick on a flat surface, like the back of a dinner plate or baking sheet. Allow the dough to cool.

When the dough has cooled, loosen the edges with a knife and peel it off. Cut it into triangles or squares. Heat 2 inches of oil in a large sauté pan or deep fryer, not too hot. Fry the pieces a batch at a time, turning them to cook evenly. They should be golden brown and slightly puffed. Drain the Panelle on paper towels. This makes enough to serve 6 as part of a Fritto Misto.

Panelle.

Uova alla Monacale *Friars' Eggs*

Béchamel

   3 tablespoons butter

   4 tablespoons flour

   1 cup milk

   Salt

   Black pepper

   ✤

   6 hard-boiled eggs

   ¹/₂ cup flour

   Salt

   Black pepper

   1 egg, beaten with 1 teaspoon water

   1 cup fine breadcrumbs

   Oil, for frying

Melt the butter for the béchamel in a small saucepan and remove it from the heat. Add the 4 tablespoons flour, whisking to incorporate it. Put the pan back on the stove and add the milk gradually, continuing to whisk to prevent lumps. Continue to whisk the béchamel as it thickens. It should be very dense. Season with salt and pepper.

Peel the hard-boiled eggs, cut them in half lengthwise, and remove the yolk. Mix the egg yolks with some of the béchamel, fill the eggs with this mixture, and put them back together. There will be some béchamel left over. Cover, refrigerate, and use it for another purpose.

Put the ¹/₂ cup flour in a shallow bowl and season it with salt and pepper. Pour the beaten egg in another bowl. Put the breadcrumbs in a third. Dip each filled egg in flour, egg, and breadcrumbs. Set aside until all are done.

Pour enough oil to float the eggs in a deep fryer or a very large sauté pan. Heat the oil until it sizzles when tested with an egg. Fry the eggs, turning occasionally, until golden. Do not crowd the pan. Drain on paper towels and serve hot. This serves 6 as part of a Fritto Misto.

Fritto Misto may sound easy, but it is a challenge to have everything ready at once, even if you have several big pans on the fire. And you can't reheat fried food—it's bad for your stomach, not to mention that it doesn't taste half as good as when freshly fried. Mario sends each batch of *Fritto Misto* to the table as soon as it is done. Agostina Farina, who cooks for me in Mondello, puts hers in a warm oven until it is all ready. You can do this too, but the fried food goes a little soft and is not quite as good as when just made.

Sicilians are very particular about their *frittura* (fried food). Even at the humblest *friggitoria*, you will see customers waiting for the hot *frittura* just out of the pan. The pieces lying on the counter go to those who don't care or don't know any better.

Meat and Fish

We eat a lot of cold dishes in summer. When I lived with my husband Vences's family in the Palazzo Mazzarino in Palermo, summers were so very hot, you really could not eat anything warm. The sea breeze I was used to in Mondello did not follow me all the way into town.

One of the dishes we often had was *Vitello Tonné*. It's a northern Italian dish, but my in-laws had lived in Rome and acquired a taste for it. I still do it in my home, and everyone in the family loves it.

A word about *maionese*. We have always made it with raw egg, and it has never caused any problems, perhaps because our chickens are healthier than those from factory farms. If you are worried about the risk of salmonella, I suggest you substitute a commercial mayonnaise.

VITELLO TONNÉ *Veal in Tuna Sauce*

Agglassato di Vitello

One 2-pound veal roast, top round or veal tip, tied

1/4 cup olive oil

1 medium carrot, coarsely chopped

1 stalk celery, coarsely chopped

1 medium onion, sliced

Salt

Black pepper

2 cups white wine

1 bay leaf

Maionese

1 egg yolk, at room temperature

Pinch of salt

2 cups vegetable oil

2 to 3 tablespoons freshly squeezed lemon juice

1 tablespoon white wine vinegar

❧

One 6 1/2-ounce can albacore tuna packed in olive oil, rinsed and drained

1 1/2 tablespoons capers, rinsed

Lemon slices, for garnish

Capers, rinsed, for garnish

Chopped parsley, for garnish

For the agglassato, choose a pot just large enough to hold the roast. Put the roast
and the olive oil in the pot and brown the meat on all sides. Add the carrot, celery,
and onion and season to taste with salt and pepper. Add the wine and enough water
to come three-fourths of the way up the veal. Add the bay leaf. Bring to a boil,
reduce the heat, and simmer, skimming any foam that rises to the surface. Cover and
cook over low heat until the veal is tender, about 2 hours. Remove the veal and set it
aside to cool. Strain the sauce and refrigerate or freeze it to save for another purpose.

To make the maionese, put the egg yolk in a medium bowl and stir until smooth.
Add a pinch of salt and stir for 1 minute. Stir in the oil in small quantities until the
sauce is pale yellow and thick. When it is very thick, add some of the lemon juice.
Continue adding oil until you have used it all. Season to taste with vinegar and additional salt.

To make the tuna sauce, put 1 cup of the maionese in a food processor with the tuna and capers and process until smooth. Blend in more maionese to make as much sauce as you will need to cover the meat. Taste and correct the seasonings. Refrigerate any leftover maionese to use for another purpose.

Slice the veal $^1/_2$ inch thick. Spread some of the sauce on the bottom of a serving platter large enough to contain all the veal slices in one layer. Add the veal and cover with additional tuna sauce. Garnish with lemon slices, capers, and parsley. Cover and refrigerate the platter for several hours. This dish should be served cold. This serves 6 as a main course.

Mario often makes a chicken dish, *Pollo in Gelatina* (Chicken in Aspic), in summer. He boils a chicken with herbs and aromatics, removes the skin and bones, and covers the meat with *Gelatina Piccante*. He puts very fine julienne strips of red pepper and carrot and sometimes slices of boiled ham with the chicken for color and added flavor. Unlike some other cold chicken dishes I have tasted, it is never insipid. I think that's partly because our chickens have lots of flavor, since they are left to range free and are killed just a day or two before cooking.

Something else that is good to serve on a hot day is a big platter of *Carne Fredda Mista* (Mixed Cold Meats), with slices of beef *agglassato*, boiled ham, prosciutto, cold chicken, bresaola, and so on. We would serve these with either homemade mayonnaise or a vinaigrette with chopped pickles.

Sarde a Beccafico are very appetizing in summer, and they make a very attractive dish. Just be careful not to break the tails off when you are cleaning the fish. You can even stuff the sardines, arrange them in the baking dish, and refrigerate them until shortly before serving. Bring the dish to room temperature before baking them.

There are several stories about the origin of the name of this dish. Some people say it comes from the fact that the stuffed sardines look like the *beccafico*, a little bird that grows chubby from eating figs.

SARDE A BECCAFICO *Stuffed Sardines*

Ripieno di Passoli e Pinoli

1 medium red onion, very finely chopped

¹/₂ cup olive oil

³/₄ cup breadcrumbs

5 tablespoons dried currants, soaked in water for 5 minutes if very dry

5 tablespoons pine nuts

¹/₂ cup minced parsley

¹/₄ cup mixed lemon and orange juices

Sugar (optional)

Salt

Black pepper

⌁

2 pounds whole fresh sardines, scaled, cleaned, heads removed, split, and boned

¹/₂ lemon, sliced ¹/₄ inch thick

¹/₂ orange, sliced ¹/₄ inch thick

12 fresh or 6 dried bay leaves, broken in half

Sauté the onion in the olive oil until just golden, 2 to 3 minutes. Stir in the breadcrumbs and cook for 2 to 3 minutes to toast the crumbs. Remove from the heat. Add the currants, pine nuts, and parsley. Taste the lemon-and-orange-juice mixture and add some sugar if it seems too sour. Stir into the filling mixture, season to taste with salt and pepper, and mix well. Let this cool.

Preheat the oven to 375°F. Oil an 8-inch-square baking dish.

Fill each sardine with about 1¹/₂ teaspoons of filling. Roll each fish, going from the head to the tail. Place the sardines with their tails sticking up, all in the same direction and close together, in the baking dish. Sprinkle them with the remaining filling. Place the slices of lemon and orange and the bay leaves decoratively around the dish, at the sides or in between the sardines.

Bake for 15 to 20 minutes, until tender. Serve warm or at room temperature. This serves 4 to 6 people as a first course.

If we have bought too many sardines and there are some left, we might have a few *Sarde Fritte* (Fried Sardines) with a glass of wine. For this dish, the sardines are butterflied and boned, then steeped in vinegar for an hour or so. When ready, they are coated with semolina flour and deep-fried. Usually, we plan ahead to have *Sarde Fritte* as a second course.

The filling we use for the sardines we also use for *Involtini di Pesce Spada*. We have these quite often in summer. They are ideal in hot weather, very light and fresh tasting, and as with *Sarde a Beccafico,* the basic preparation can be done ahead.

INVOLTINI DI PESCE SPADA *Swordfish Rolls*

12 swordfish slices, less than ¼ inch thick (about 2 pounds)
Salt
Ripieno di Passoli e Pinoli (page 141)
¼ cup olive oil
14 to 16 bay leaves

Ask your fishmonger to cut the swordfish slices for you. The slices must be very thin in order to be flexible. If the slices are not thin enough, put them between 2 sheets of wax paper and carefully pound with the side of a rolling pin until you get the desired thinness. Sprinkle the swordfish with salt and set aside.

Preheat the oven to 375°F. Lightly oil an 8×12-inch baking dish.

Place the swordfish slices on a flat surface. Put about 1 tablespoon of the filling in the middle of each slice. Roll it up to form a roll about 2×1 inch in size. Place the rolls in the baking dish and sprinkle with the remaining filling and the olive oil. Put a bay leaf between each roll and at the end of each row. Bake for 12 to 15 minutes, or until the fish is opaque and firm. Serve warm or at room temperature. This serves 6 as a main course.

Sweets

When the *zucca lunga* gets old and is inedible, there is still something to make with it, the famous *Marmellata di Zucca* (Squash Preserves). I say famous because the nuns—the few who are left in the convents in Sicily—mix it with pistachios and put it into some of their famous little sweets.

I think the nuns decided to preserve the squash when they couldn't eat it all before it went to seed. In fact, the original recipe calls for an old *zucca*, but the first time I made it, I used a young one, and it made very good preserves. When I told a friend of mine who knows everything about these matters, she scolded me, saying the *marmellata* can be done only with an old *zucca*. I went back to work and picked an enormous one; now it was the gardener scolding me because he had been saving it for seed. I took the squash into the kitchen and started cutting it. I couldn't do it by myself, not even with my sharpest knife, because the skin was as tough as bark. I can't tell you what hard work it was. Now I use young but not-too-tender squash.

To make *Marmellata di Zucca,* I peel the squash and cut it into quarter-inch dice. (I used to do this by hand, but now I use the julienne blade of the food processor.) Then I put the diced squash in a pot with an equal amount of sugar by weight, and cook it over very low heat, trying not to stir it—otherwise the sugar goes crazy and either caramelizes or crystallizes. It takes forty minutes to an hour for the syrup to thicken. When the syrup is thick and the fruit transparent, I put the *marmellata* in a sterilized jar, which is left open. The preserves crystallize on top in a few days. My technique may not be quite the same as that of the nuns, but the preserves are very good.

The most common homemade dessert using *Marmellata di Zucca* is *Biancomangiare.* It is extremely sweet. My father loves it, and I usually make it for him.

The marzipan heart was fashioned by Maria Grammatico. Sicilian almonds are buttery and full of flavor. I fill Biancomangiare (page 146) with pistachios and my own zucchini preserves.

BIANCOMANGIARE *Blancmange*

2 tablespoons shelled unsalted pistachios
2 tablespoons Marmellata di Zucca (page 143) or finely chopped candied citron
Ground cinnamon
¹/₄ cup cornstarch
2 cups milk
¹/₄ cup sugar
Chopped pistachios, for garnish

Blanch the pistachios in boiling water for 3 to 5 minutes, until the skins are loosened. Drain and peel the pistachios by rubbing them in a towel. Cut the pistachios into very small pieces. Mix them together with the marmellata. Set aside. Sprinkle the bottom of a 4-cup bowl with cinnamon and set aside.

Put the cornstarch in a strainer over a saucepan and pour the milk through it several times until all the cornstarch is dissolved. Place over medium heat and add the sugar, whisking constantly. Bring to a boil, continuing to whisk constantly, and boil for 1 minute. Remove from the heat and pour the custard immediately into the prepared bowl, filling it two-thirds full. Add the pistachios and preserves in a layer. Cover with the remaining custard and smooth the top with a spatula. Let the pudding cool. It will thicken to the consistency of a very thick béchamel.

Refrigerate only in hot weather. When ready to serve, unmold and garnish with chopped pistachios around the edges. This serves 4.

Zuccata (candied squash) is made with yet another variety of summer squash, which is grown under contract to the confectioners. This squash is shaped like an oval watermelon with very pale green skin. It weighs anywhere from six to twenty pounds. *Zuccata* is translucent, golden or light green in color, and very sweet. It is very finely chopped and used for filling *pasticcini* (pastries), especially the traditional almond pastries. The fancier pieces of *zuccata* are called *capelli d'angelo* (angel's hair). They are as thick as your finger with sugar all around. *Capelli d'angelo* are served with coffee, as are *Cotognata*, *Torrone di Noci*, and *Biscotti Regina*.

A couple of years ago, I was able to get some seeds and plant them. The vines were prolific, and soon I had a house full of *zucche*. It's a good thing, too, because I had to try over and over again before I was able to make my own *zuccata* and *capelli d'angelo*. It's a long process that takes days of salting, followed by days of sugaring, before it is ready to eat.

Sometimes I wish the nuns would give me all their recipes for their *zuccate*. Two hundred years ago there were many convents producing sweets, but now there are only a few, and as the old nuns die, many secrets die with them. Mary Simeti, who wrote so eloquently in *On Persephone's Island* of the *grappolo d'uva*, a life-size cluster of pale-green grapes made of almond and pistachio marzipan and filled with *Marmellata di Zucca* flavored with cinnamon, later learned that the nun whose specialty it was had died suddenly. "There is no one else in the convent who knows her secrets," Mary writes, "so the bunch of grapes is gone forever. Another chapter in Sicilian culinary history has come to a close."

Forming the *acini* (individual grapes) is so very tricky that it must have taken all the prayers and patience of a nun to make them. I would love to know how it was done.

The nuns still make the traditional *Trionfo di Gola* (Triumph of Gluttony), another of the monumental convent sweets. There are several versions of this cone-shaped confection. Usually *Pan di Spagna* is layered with a *Biancomangiare*-type custard with pistachios and *Marmellata di Zucca*. The cake is coated with preserves (apricot and pistachio are two kinds I've heard of), then covered with *Pasta Reale* and decorated with candied fruit.

Maria Grammatico, who has a pastry shop in Erice, makes many of the traditional convent sweets. One day Maria came to Regaleali to show Mario and a group of visiting chefs her way with marzipan. First she made *Pasta Reale*. She piled finely ground almonds on the counter, made a well in the center, and mixed in some sugar and water. Then she passed the marzipan through a meat grinder to make a finer dough and kneaded it again, sprinkling the marble surface with confectioners' sugar to keep the dough from sticking. When the *Pasta Reale* was ready, she made some marzipan fruits, using molds she had brought with her, and painted them. Everyone watched wide-eyed and openmouthed. Then, when we all thought she had finished, with her wonderfully expert hands she made a couple of rosebuds with leaves—they looked just like a brooch—and offered them to me.

In western Sicily, molded marzipan fruit is called *frutta di Martorana* because, supposedly, it was invented in the convent of the Martorana in Palermo. Besides fruits and vegetables, there are molds for *Conchiglie delle Monache* (Nuns' Shells). The shell is a common motif in western Sicily. You can see real shells embedded in the walks of the cloister of San Giovanni in Palermo and a sculpted one shelters the head of the Virgin in a grotto there. And, of course, there is the shell in the famous depiction of Aphrodite rising from the sea, a mythological event that supposedly occurred within sight of Erice. I have made the *conchiglie* without a mold, though, just two shell-shaped pieces of *Pasta Reale* enclosing a spoonful of my *Marmellata di Zucca* mixed with some chopped pistachios.

I like to make marzipan the same way as Maria, but some people find it easier to do in the food processor, which gives very good results. You still have to knead the dough by hand until it is smooth and let it rest before trying to mold it or roll it out.

Pasta Reale *Marzipan*

2 cups blanched whole almonds (10 ounces)
2 cups sugar
3 tablespoons water
Confectioners' sugar, for dusting
2 or 3 drops green food coloring (optional)

Put the almonds in a food processor and process them until crumbly. Add the sugar and process until combined. Add the water and pulse to mix. Knead the marzipan on a work surface, dusted with confectioners' sugar, until smooth, about 3 minutes. Add the food coloring, if desired. Form the marzipan into a 2×8-inch log. Wrap it in plastic and refrigerate until you're ready to use it. This makes about 1 3/4 pounds of marzipan.

‖ *Nuts* ‖

It should not be surprising that so many of our traditional sweets are based on almonds. They grow in abundance all over Sicily, including Regaleali. The trees that were in bloom in February bear fruit in June. Some nuts are picked then, but most are left on the tree. By the end of August, the taste changes, becoming crisper with a stronger flavor.

The almond harvest takes place in mid-September. Sheets are spread out under the trees, and the branches of the trees are beaten with a stick to bring down the nuts. As the nuts dry on the sheets in the sun, the outer green shell opens and falls apart. The nuts are then removed from the outer shell and stored.

The almonds we pick at the end of June are watery and tender. At my parents' table, these early almonds are served in fruit salad or at the end of the meal, peeled and floating in a glass bowl of salted water. We nibble them while waiting for my father to finish smoking his Toscano, a very popular, very smelly cigar.

Later in the season we make brittle, which is served at the end of the meal or with coffee, or *Mandorle Fritte* (Fried Almonds) to have with drinks before dinner. For the fried almonds, you combine some blanched almonds with olive oil (about a cup and a half of nuts in a half cup of oil) in a sauté pan and cook, stirring constantly, for about five minutes, until golden. Then you remove the nuts with a slotted spoon and drain them on paper towels. Sprinkle the nuts with lots of coarse salt and pour them into jars, cover, and cool. Give a jar to a good friend.

In addition to the almond, the pistachio is used extensively in our pastries and sweets.

We can never make enough Biscotti Regina (page 150). They disappear in no time.

Though some pistachios are cultivated, especially near Bronte on the slopes of Etna, most are imported, so they are expensive. Despite the cost, however, no one would think of omitting the pistachio in a traditional sweet. It adds a very special flavor and, of course, its extraordinary green color. There is no substitute.

More plentiful are pine nuts, which are used in many kinds of *biscotti* and in cooking. The marriage between pine nuts and dried currants is very Sicilian; its origins are lost in the mists of time, possibly dating back to pre–Arabian days.

There is another kind of brittle that is made with sesame seeds; it is called *cubbaita di giuggiulena* in dialect. But mostly sesame seeds are used on bread and some pastries, such as *Biscotti Regina*. If you make the *biscotti*, take care to handle the dough as little as possible; it will get tough if overworked.

Biscotti Regina dough can also be used to make *Biscotti a Rombo* (Diamond-shaped Cookies). They can be plain or you can knead in some ground almonds, pine nuts, or pistachios or dried currants or raisins. Roll out the dough and cut it into diamond shapes. Bake the cookies for fifteen to twenty minutes in a 350°F. oven. These cookies are dusted with confectioners' sugar. The children love them.

BISCOTTI REGINA *The Queen's Cookies*

5 cups flour
Pinch of salt
1 cup sugar
1/2 pound butter, cut into 1/2-inch dice
1 large egg, at room temperature
4 large egg yolks, at room temperature
4 egg whites
1/2 cup water
2 to 2 1/2 cups unhulled sesame seeds

Pour the flour, salt, and sugar onto a work surface or into a bowl and mix thoroughly. Work the butter into the flour until the mixture is crumbly. Make a well in the center, add the egg and egg yolks, and stir to blend. Knead just until the dough is soft. Wrap the dough in plastic and refrigerate it for at least 30 minutes.

Divide the dough into 6 pieces and roll each piece into a long rope, about 1 inch thick. Cut the rope into 1-inch pieces.

Preheat the oven to 350°F. Line a baking sheet with foil or parchment paper.

Beat the egg whites with a fork, adding the water, in a medium bowl. Put the sesame seeds in another bowl. Drop the biscotti in the egg wash, about 20 at a time, then lift them out, letting the egg drip between your fingers, and transfer them to the bowl with the sesame seeds. Shake to coat the pieces completely with seeds. Form each piece into an olive shape, pressing the seeds into the dough. Place them close together, nearly touching, on the baking sheet. Bake for about 30 minutes, until nicely browned. If the biscotti need additional crisping, turn off the oven and leave them for about 5 more minutes, until crisp. Cool on a rack. Store the biscotti in an airtight container. This makes about 120 cookies.

Walnuts are not ready to be picked until September, but I mention them in summer because we always pick some green ones on June 24, the feast of San Giovanni, to make *Nocino* (Walnut Liqueur). We are tradition-bound to pick the nuts on that day and none other. To make the *Nocino*, we cut each nut in four, and put it into a jar of alcohol with sugar, cinnamon, cloves, lemon peel, and some water. The jar is left in the sun for forty days. Then the brew is filtered and put away until I Morti (All Souls' Day, November 2), when we drink it to honor the dead.

L'Autunno

FALL

As summer ends and fall approaches, the entire

countryside seems to want to make its final offering. The abundance

of midsummer gives way to the urgency of the vendemmia (grape harvest).

This is always a time of high emotion. Wine making is an enormous gamble.

Every year there are surprises, and with all the new varieties we've

planted in the last few years, it has become even more of a

challenge than before. With wine, the stakes are high, and no matter how

much man reduces the risks, nature keeps piling them on. Rain or

no rain; the scirocco, the hot wind from Africa; hail; frost; and so on. Father

Ronald Marino from Brooklyn sometimes shows up at Regaleali for

the vendemmia. His presence is always a welcome one. As my brother, Lucio,

says, "We need Father's intervention, because only He decides."

NOWADAYS THE HARVEST BEGINS in mid-August, when for two weeks the Pinot Noir and Chardonnay grapes are picked for the sparkling wines. It reaches a peak in mid-September and goes on until mid-October. The Cabernet Sauvignon is picked at the beginning of September. The native varieties are picked last. The peak of activity comes in mid-September, when more than a hundred men from the nearby villages are working in the vineyards. In the old days, they worked "from star to star," as it used to be said, but now the workday is much shorter.

Vincenzo Curcio organizes and supervises the harvest, but he doesn't need to say much. He has taught the men how to follow the timeless rituals of the *vendemmia*. They plod up and down the rows of vines, systematically clipping the bunches of grapes and dropping them into their buckets. As the men move quietly and rhythmically through the vineyards, their toil appears effortless.

When the buckets are full, they are emptied into a gondola that is hauled through the vineyards by a small tractor. In less than an hour, the grapes are at the winery for the crush. When the grapes arrive, they are dumped into a stainless-steel *tramoggia* (stemmer). The smell that rises out of the *tramoggia* is incredible, a mixture of grape and soil that I can't describe except to say it's heavenly.

For the Regaleali Bianco, the grapes—Sauvignon Tasca, Inzolia, and Cataratto—get a soft press after stemming, and the must is transferred to stainless-steel cooling tanks. When the sediment has settled, it is filtered and cleaned and added back to the clear must, which undergoes controlled-temperature fermentation for about ten days. Then the wine is returned to normal vats for a final fermentation, the so-called malolactic conversion.

Regaleali Rosato is made in a similar manner, but with red grapes, Nerello Mascalese and Calabrese, two other native varieties, and the must comes into limited contact with the skins. We are very pleased with the Rosato. Unfortunately, some people think rosé wine is a mixture of red and white wines—which of course it is not.

Regaleali Rosso is made with Perricone and Nero d'Avola grapes. After the grapes are stemmed, the must and the skins are moved to stainless-steel vats, where the temperature is kept at the fermentation point for several days. Afterward the wine is aged in French oak.

In addition to these classic white, rosé, and red wines, we produce some very special wines. Rosso del Conte, for example, is a big wine, full-bodied and aromatic. It appeals to a lot of wine lovers because of its unusual taste, so unlike other Sicilian reds. It dates back to 1955 when Paolo Camporeale, then my sister Costanza's fiancé, offered my father a glass of Chateauneuf-du-Pape. It was, as the French say, *un coup de foudre* (love at first sip). Later, when my father started the wine business, he decided to try to create a similar wine. He chose his best barrel—chestnut at the time—and picked the best Perricone and Nero d'Avola grapes from the finest vineyard, the Vigneto di San Lucio, near Case Vecchie. He aged the wine for five years, first in barrels and then in bottles. When the first lot was released, the wine was an instant success. Now Lucio is dreaming of making his own Regaleali red.

Our latest red wine is the Cabernet Sauvignon di Regaleali. It is made from Cabernet Sauvignon grapes grown in the Vigneto di San Francesco and processed the traditional way with skin contact. The wine is aged in oak *barriques* for several months.

Our latest white wine is called Villa Tasca, after the family's historic villa in Palermo. It is a blend of Sauvignon Tasca and Inzolia, and it is made in a very particular fashion. The must and the skins are kept in contact for several hours, then softly pressed. The result is a dry wine with enhanced bouquet.

Nozze d'Oro, which was my father's present to my mother on their fiftieth wedding anniversary, is a white wine with a certain exotic quality. It, too, is made from Sauvignon Tasca and Inzolia grapes. When it was first released, the entire stock was quickly sold out. Instead of doing it only for the year of my parents' golden wedding anniversary as was originally intended, we decided to go on making it. It sells out every year.

Now my father is preparing the Nozze di Diamante dessert wine, both wine and label still top secret. It will be his present to my mother on their sixtieth, or diamond, wedding anniversary, June 3, 1995.

The Hunt

The end of August marks *l'apertura di caccia* (the opening of the hunt). All the men—grandfathers, fathers, sons, husbands, family friends—used to go out before sunrise or at sunset and come back loaded with rabbits, hundreds of them. This was a time of feasting for all. Everyone could make big meals; sometimes we would even roast a rabbit for

Grapes are still gathered the ancient way, but the handpress is only a memento. A few vines are trained in the traditional manner; they look like little trees. Most are espaliered. Lucio, my brother, checks some bottles in the courtyard. Enologist Giuseppe Cavaleri holds red wine to the light. From high atop the stainless-steel wine vats, the Madonna surveys Regaleali.

breakfast when the men came back from the hunt. Nowadays there is very little game, and we seldom get the opportunity to eat wild rabbit. I think it's because with the winery we work the land all year round and the rabbits are constantly being chased from their burrows.

Lucio still hunts, but he goes away from Regaleali to hunt birds, partridge and woodcock especially. He often comes back with a bag full of snails instead of a bag full of game, to the joy of those of us—he and I included—who love them. *Attuppatelli Soffritti in Padella* (Snails Sicilian Style) is the easiest and best way to prepare the brown ones gathered in autumn. Purge the snails by leaving them in a basket with nothing but bran to eat for three days. Wash the snails and put them in a sauté pan with a little oil, breadcrumbs, and lots of chopped garlic and parsley and fry them for about twenty minutes. To eat the snails, pry them out of their shells with a toothpick and dip bread in the juices.

Nowadays when Mario makes his *Pasticcio di Caccia*, he has to go to a special purveyor for the fresh hare and game birds (pheasant, quail, snipe, and doves) he needs. In winter he uses frozen game. He removes the feathers or fur from the fresh game and cleans the animal. He cuts it up if it is large—a hare, for instance. Mario makes *Pasticcio di Caccia* for Christmas or when we have special guests. He likes to garnish the plate with pheasant feathers.

PASTICCIO DI CACCIA *Game Pâté*

One 2½- to 3-pound hare or rabbit, cut into 8 pieces

One 2½-pound pheasant

Three 6-ounce quail

One 1-pound pigeon or squab

Salt

Black pepper

¾ cup olive oil

3 large red onions, minced

½ pound boiled ham, chopped

½ pound pancetta, chopped

About 2½ pounds butter, softened

4 pounds chicken livers, cleaned

6 garlic cloves, minced

1 cup white wine

8 cups Gelatina Piccante (page 165), cooled but not set

Season the hare, pheasant, quail, and pigeon with salt and pepper and put them in several large pans with the olive oil. Sauté the game for about 10 to 15 minutes, until it is browned. Add the onions, ham, and pancetta, and continue sautéing until the game meat is tender. Take the meat from the pans and allow it to cool. Puree the onion, ham, and pancetta and set aside. Remove the meat from the bone and cut it into ½-inch dice. Return the meat to one of the pans and set aside.

Melt 6 tablespoons of the butter in a medium sauté pan. Season the chicken livers with salt and pepper and put them into the pan. Add the garlic. Cook the chicken livers over medium heat for 3 to 4 minutes, or until cooked through. Add the wine to the pan and cook 1 to 2 minutes more. Remove the livers from the heat and let them cool. Pass the chicken livers through a food mill, or puree them in a food processor and pass them through a sieve, using a spatula to push the mixture through.

Weigh the chicken-liver mixture and add an equal amount of the remaining softened butter. Mix and knead until this mousse is thoroughly uniform in color and texture. Refrigerate it to thicken until its consistency is like that of cold mashed potatoes. Fold in the diced meat and the onion mixture.

Butter two 6-cup or one 12-cup pâté mold. Line with plastic wrap. Spoon in the mixture. Cover the pâté with plastic wrap and refrigerate it overnight.

Pour a thin layer of the cooled gelatina on a platter and refrigerate it until it is set. Dip the mold in hot water and unmold the pâté onto the platter. Remove the plastic wrap. Pour a thin layer of gelatina over the pâté and refrigerate it until set. Continue to do this until the layer of gelatina is about ⅛ to ¼ inch thick. If you have some left over, cut it into neat pieces and use them to decorate the plate. Serve cold or at room temperature. One 6-cup pâté mold will serve 10 to 12 as a first course.

People who grew up in the country eating wild rabbit would never eat a farmed one. They would feel betrayed at the first bite. The way we cook rabbit, the most popular way now that it has become so rare—at least compared with the enormous numbers we used to have—is *Coniglio Arrosto* (Roast Rabbit). We grill or roast the rabbit for about forty minutes, basting it from time to time with a sauce of salt, pepper, oregano, garlic, vinegar or lemon juice, and olive oil. This we eat immediately—always being careful not to break a tooth on a piece of shot.

Mario.

The Cooks

When we were children, the family used to spend long periods in the country at the time of the wheat harvest and the grape harvest or whenever my parents felt we needed to get out in the fresh air, like after a flu. My parents traveled with maids and nannies but no cook. My grandfather's cook, Ciccioilcuoco (Ciccio the Cook), would never have tolerated a rival in the kitchen. My grandfather, however, was welcome. The two of them spent a lot of time together inventing new dishes, and the food was delicious.

Ciccioilcuoco was a funny little round man with a perfectly round head. He had a shiny mustache and just one lock of hair, which he combed around his whole head, ending with a spit curl at his left ear. Costanza and I were thin and frail little girls and often didn't want to eat. That's when Ciccioilcuoco would come on the scene, carrying a pot lid in each hand. He would bang them together like cymbals, and when we opened our mouths in awe, in went the food.

Giovannino, the old *monzù*, worked mostly at the Villa Tasca in Palermo, coming to Regaleali only for special events when he was needed. When my father was a little boy, Giovannino taught him how to ride and how to build and fly a kite. He had joined the Tasca household in 1914 when my father's uncles and their mother, Nonna Annetta, were still alive. When she died (just before I was born; I was named after her), Zio Alessandro, the eldest brother, who was very stingy, said he could not afford a *monzù*, but the others insisted on keeping Giovannino on. As the uncles died off one by one, my father and mother inherited Giovannino.

He was a hard taskmaster in the kitchen (ask Mario), but he loved us children and liked to prepare our favorite dishes—what is called "comfort food" these days—as well as the elaborate *monzù* dishes for which he was famed. One of those comfort dishes I still like to have when Mario makes it is *Latte Fritto*.

LATTE FRITTO *Fried Custard*

Crema

2 cups milk

$^1/_3$ cup cornstarch

2 eggs, at room temperature

4 egg yolks, at room temperature

$^3/_4$ cup sugar

Grated peel of 1 lemon

2 teaspoons vanilla extract

4 tablespoons butter

⌘

Oil, for frying

$^1/_4$ cup flour, sifted

2 eggs, beaten with 2 teaspoons water

$1^1/_2$ cups fine breadcrumbs

1 cup sugar mixed with 1 teaspoon cinnamon

Mix $^1/_2$ cup of the milk with the cornstarch in a large bowl, whisking to dissolve. Beat the 2 eggs and the 4 egg yolks and add them to the cornstarch and milk. Combine the remaining milk and the sugar in a medium saucepan and bring to a boil. Remove the pan from the heat. Whisk some of the hot-milk mixture into the milk, cornstarch, and eggs, and once this egg mixture is warmed, pour in the remaining milk.

Strain the crema back into the saucepan and add the grated lemon peel. Bring to a boil and cook for 30 seconds to 1 minute, until the mixture thickens. Remove it from the heat. Add the vanilla and butter and stir to blend.

Butter an 8×12-inch baking dish. Pour the crema into the dish, spreading it out evenly. Put a buttered sheet of plastic wrap on the surface and refrigerate it until set, at least 2 to 3 hours.

Cut the crema into $1^1/_2$- to 2-inch circles, squares, or diamonds. Dredge each piece in flour, dip into the egg, and coat with breadcrumbs. Set aside until all are done. Heat 1 inch of oil in a large, deep sauté pan. Fry the pieces in batches without crowding the pan until golden brown. Drain on paper towels. Roll each piece in the cinnamon sugar. Serve warm. This dessert serves 10 to 12 people.

It always amazes me that those artists of the kitchen, who were so moody and temperamental, could be as patient as they were with children. Even now, when my grandson, Ruggero, comes to visit, Mario wraps him in an enormous apron and gives him a boiled potato to peel or a piece of dough to make cookies. It is really funny to see the two of them in the kitchen, Mario beaming all over the place and Ruggero looking solemn and proud.

One more thing I want to say about Giovannino: for my wedding he re-created a most extraordinary dish from an old family recipe. He made chicken medallions with truffles in aspic and served them in pasta baskets decorated with flowers dipped in wax. Mario did the same for my daughter's wedding.

You can make these *Cesti di Fiori di Cera* (Baskets with Waxed Flowers) yourself. It's complicated but fun to do, and you can use them over and over again. For the base, spread a layer of sticky, overcooked rice on a serving plate. Break pieces of raw perciatelli in half and stick them, one by one, into the rice. Do this at such an angle that the pieces cross in the middle and meet at the top, like a lattice. The basket will stand about three and a half inches high. Take a length of silver thread and tie the perciatelli here and there where the pieces meet in the middle. Dip flowers in paraffin. When they are stiff, weave the stems into the lattice. Fill the basket with whatever you want. Pâté is nice.

Giovannino used to boast that he used twenty-two pounds of liver to make one pound of pâté. Mario's pâtés aren't that rich, but they are exquisite, especially his *Spuma di Fegatini,* flavored with Marsala, one of Sicily's most famous wines.

SPUMA DI FEGATINI *Chicken Liver Mousse*

4 tablespoons butter

4 tablespoons margarine

1 small stalk celery, coarsely chopped

1 small carrot, coarsely chopped

1 small onion, coarsely chopped

1¼ pounds chicken livers, cleaned

½ cup Marsala

Béchamel

4 tablespoons butter

1 heaping tablespoon flour

1 cup milk

Salt

Black pepper

↫

4 cups Gelatina Piccante (recipe follows), cooled but not set

Parsley sprigs, for garnish

Melt half the butter and half the margarine in a sauté pan and sauté the vegetables until they soften. Add the chicken livers and cook until they are firm and well cooked. Add the Marsala, stirring to blend. Transfer the mixture to a food processor, add the remaining butter and margarine, and puree. Set aside.

For the béchamel, melt the 4 tablespoons of butter in a small saucepan and remove from the heat. Stir in the flour and put the pan back on the heat. Add the milk gradually, whisking to prevent lumps from forming. Continue to cook, whisking constantly, until the béchamel thickens. Season to taste with salt and pepper.

Add the puree to the béchamel and mix well. Pour the mixture into an oiled 4-cup mold. Cover with plastic wrap and refrigerate until solid.

Pour a thin layer of cooled gelatina on a platter and put it in the refrigerator to set. Unmold the spuma and place it on the layer of gelatina. Pour a thin layer of gelatina over the spuma and return the platter to the refrigerator. Continue to do this until the layer of gelatina is ⅛ to ¼ inch thick. Garnish with parsley and serve. This serves 10 to 12 as a first course.

A veil of Marsala-flavored gelatina coats Mario's Pasticcio di Caccia (page 158).

GELATINA PICCANTE *Aspic*

2 envelopes unflavored gelatin

1 cup white wine

¹/₂ cup white wine vinegar

¹/₄ cup Marsala

2¹/₂ cups Consomme (page 224) or 2 beef or chicken bouillon cubes dissolved in 2¹/₂
cups water

Soften the gelatin in ¹/₂ cup of the wine. Pour the remaining wine, vinegar, and Marsala into a separate quart measure, and add enough of the Consomme to make 4 cups. Heat 1 cup of the liquid and add the softened gelatin, stirring until it is dissolved. Pour this hot liquid back into the quart measure and stir to blend. Set it aside to cool, then refrigerate to set. This makes 4 cups of gelatina.

The Gardens

The gardens are full of color in fall. Large purple eggplants ripen beneath the plants' hairy leaves. The vivid green, red, and yellow of sweet and hot peppers compete with fall's own flower, the chrysanthemum. We even make a special salad combining chrysanthemum petals and kohlrabi. Tomatoes hang on the almost withered plants, and behind the tomato patch, half-hidden by their crumpled gray-green leaves, are the green cauliflowers.

We always prepare some cauliflower, which western Sicilians call *broccoli* (they call broccoli *sparacelli*), for salad. The first very tender florets can be eaten raw; later we cook them first. If Mario is making a *Fritto Misto,* he's almost certain to include *Broccoli in Pastella* (Batter-fried Cauliflower). The batter is just an egg, a cup of flour, and a pinch of salt, with enough water to thin it to the consistency of cream. Zucchini flowers can also be dipped in this type of batter and fried.

We make a gratin with the green cauliflower and our own oil-cured black olives, *Broccoli con Olive Nere.* Some people like the dish topped with *tuma* (curd cheese); you can use fresh mozzarella instead. I love the cheese topping. You can substitute white cauliflower, Swiss chard, *broccoletti di rapa,* or other flavorful greens for the green cauliflower.

BROCCOLI CON OLIVE NERE *Green Cauliflower with Black Olives*

> 2 heads green cauliflower (about 2 pounds)
> 1 small onion, minced
> 1/2 cup olive oil
> 1/2 cup oil-cured black olives, pitted and sliced
> Salt
> Black pepper
> 1/2 cup grated pecorino or parmesan
> 1/2 pound mozzarella, shredded (optional)

Cut the cauliflower into 2-inch florets and boil in well-salted water until al dente, about 5 minutes, then drain. Meanwhile, sauté the onion in half the olive oil until slightly golden, 2 to 3 minutes. Remove the pan from the heat and add the olives. Set the mixture aside.

Preheat the oven to 375°F. Oil an 8×12-inch baking dish with about 1 tablespoon of the olive oil.

Spread out the cauliflower in the dish and mix in the onion-olive mixture. Add the remaining olive oil, if desired. Add salt and pepper to taste, remembering that the olives and the cheese you will be adding may be salty. Toss the cauliflower with about half of the pecorino and top with mozzarella, if desired. Sprinkle the remaining pecorino on top. Bake for about 20 to 30 minutes, until the top is nice and golden. Serve warm or at room temperature. This serves 4 to 6 as a side dish.

Like all our vegetables, green cauliflower figures in a pasta dish, *Pasta con i Broccoli Arriminati*. The traditional combination of pine nuts and currants goes very well with green cauliflower, which has a somewhat stronger flavor than the white.

PASTA CON I BROCCOLI ARRIMINATI
Pasta with Green Cauliflower, Pine Nuts, and Currants

2 heads green cauliflower (about 2 pounds)
1 medium red onion, chopped
1/4 to 1/3 cup olive oil
3 anchovy fillets
1/2 cup Salsa di Pomodoro Passata (page 114)
1 cup white wine
3 tablespoons pine nuts
3 tablespoons dried currants, soaked in water for 5 minutes if very dry
Salt
Black pepper
1 pound perciatelli

Cut the cauliflower into 1-inch florets and cook in boiling salted water until al dente, about 5 minutes. Reserve 1 cup of the cooking water and drain. Set aside.

Sauté the onion in the olive oil for 2 to 3 minutes, until just golden. Add the anchovies and mash them, then add the cauliflower with the reserved cooking water and the salsa. Add the wine, cover, and simmer until the cauliflower is tender. Stir in the pine nuts and currants. Season to taste with salt and pepper and set aside.

Cook the perciatelli in boiling salted water until tender. Drain. Gently toss with half of the cauliflower sauce. Put the remaining sauce on top. Let rest for 5 minutes before serving. This serves 4 to 6 as a pasta course.

This inspired fall dish combining green cauliflower and black olives looks good and tastes even better (page 166).

When Mario makes Pasta con i Broccoli Arriminati (page 167), he adds saffron to the sauce.

169

Since early fall in Sicily is warm and sunny, many plants continue to bear. Eggplants are still plentiful. We preserve them for the rest of the year, both in *Caponata di Melanzane* and as *Melanzane all'Aceto sott'Olio*, in vinegar and oil.

Sometimes we have an informal meal, without cooking anything. We open jars of *Melanzane all'Aceto sott'Olio, Funghi all'Aceto sott'Olio, Tonno sott'Olio, Pomodori Seccati al Sole*, and olives. The idea is to put eggplant in one corner of your dish, mushrooms in another, tuna in a third, and so on, and eat them all up with pieces of bread dipped in the olive oil in which they were preserved. This is the only kind of meal in which you put everything on the same plate. Otherwise it's severely forbidden, because you want to savor each dish.

For my father's eightieth birthday, we had a party that lasted three days with about thirty of us, all his children, grandchildren, and great-grandchildren, staying at Regaleali. One of the lunches was in my big kitchen at Case Vecchie. We had freshly baked bread with all my preserves. We put two rows of chairs around the table and the little ones were running all over the place. I can't describe the confusion. Everyone was having a good time except my father. He usually loves picnics, but he felt that this sort of meal was not serious enough for his birthday, that we should have had at least one warm dish. But then he got into the spirit of the occasion and enjoyed himself with the rest of us.

MELANZANE ALL'ACETO SOTT'OLIO *Preserved Eggplant*

4 pounds eggplant, peeled and cut into fine ($1/8$-inch) julienne
Salt
$1/4$ cup white wine vinegar
2 to 3 cups olive oil
2 small hot peppers, cut in half
2 garlic cloves, minced
2 tablespoons dried oregano

Put the eggplant in a large bowl and sprinkle it with salt and the vinegar. Place a lid on top and weight it down with several large cans. Let it stand for 24 hours.

Drain the eggplant. Put it in a clean dish towel and squeeze out all the juices. The eggplant will form a small tight mass. Place it in a clean bowl and sprinkle it with some of the oil. Add the hot peppers, garlic, and oregano and toss to combine. Spoon the mixture into sterilized jars and press to remove air pockets and to pack the eggplant. Make sure each jar has half a hot pepper in it. Cover with oil, leaving a $1/2$-inch space at the top of each jar. Seal and store for 2 months, which allows the flavors to develop. This makes about 3 pint jars.

As the weather gets cooler and appetites begin to stir, we are even more likely than ever to fry eggplant slices and put them on top of pasta and incorporate them in such dishes as *Uova a Trippa*, a casserole made with thick homemade egg crepes.

UOVA A TRIPPA *Egg Ribbons*

4 eggs
2/3 cup flour
1 cup milk
Salt
2 cups Salsa di Pomodoro Passata (page 114)
1 pound eggplant, peeled, sliced, and fried (optional)
1/2 pound fresh mozzarella or goat cheese, coarsely grated or sliced
1/2 cup grated parmesan

Beat the eggs and whisk in the flour, a little at a time. Whisk in the milk and beat to combine. Season to taste with salt.

Grease a 9-inch nonstick crepe or omelet pan with butter or oil, and put it over medium heat. When the pan is hot, pour slightly more than 1/3 cup of the batter into the pan and swirl, making a thick crepe. Cook it until the top sets, then turn it over to brown on the other side. Transfer the crepe to a plate or cool surface. Continue until all the batter is finished, adding more butter or oil as needed. Stack the crepes and cut them into 3/8-inch strips. Set aside.

Preheat the oven to 350°F. Butter or oil an 8×12-inch baking dish.

Mix the strips with two-thirds of the salsa. Spread half in the bottom of the baking dish, arrange a layer of eggplant slices on top, if you are using them, and cover with the mozzarella. Cover with the remaining strips and remaining eggplant slices, and pour the rest of the sauce on top. Sprinkle with some of the parmesan. Bake for 20 minutes, until the dish is bubbling and the cheese is starting to brown. Let it stand for 10 minutes before serving. Pass the remaining parmesan at the table. This serves 6 as a first course.

One of the special vegetables of fall is *zucca gialla* (yellow squash). It is the same one that is used in northern Italy to fill cappelletti. This squash is striped green on the outside and has orange flesh. It has a sweetish taste, like pumpkin or winter squash. *Zucca gialla* is very big, so big it is sold by the piece in the market. We like it thickly sliced and fried, either hot when just fried or cold with an onion relish called *Cipollata* on top. This dish has the sweet-and-sour taste Sicilians appreciate.

Covering food this way began as a method of preservation; supposedly it was brought to Sicily by the Arabs. We put *Cipollata* on top of all kinds of fried food besides squash— liver, cutlets, fish. You put the warm *Cipollata* on top of the fried food, whatever it is, and let the dish stand at room temperature for at least several hours, or overnight, before eating.

CIPOLLATA *Onion Topping*

4 medium red onions, sliced
2/3 cup olive oil
1 cup water
1/2 cup vinegar
1 tablespoon sugar
1 teaspoon salt
1/2 cup mint leaves

Put the onions and olive oil in a skillet and sauté for 5 minutes, until the onions are soft and clear. Cover and cook for 10 minutes longer, shaking the pan from time to time. Add the water, cover, and cook until the onions are very soft, about 8 minutes. Stir in the vinegar, sugar, salt, and mint. This makes about 1 cup of topping.

We also have cardoons in fall. What we call cardoons are the young shoots of artichokes. The cardoons of Piedmont, *gobbi*, are a different, though related, plant. All cardoons have to be trimmed and blanched first; then we use them in salads or gratins.

One of the dishes we make while we can still cook from the garden is *Regaleali Stew*. It is a rich stew that is best served in a soup bowl as *un piatto unico* (a one-dish meal).

During World War II, the family of my best friend, Sandra Ducrot, lived with us at Regaleali. Sandra's mother, Gloria, was American, and my grandfather liked to tease her. "We're having Irish stew today for lunch," he would say. "No, Cavalière Lucio," she would answer, "this is *Regaleali* stew."

The winery entrance.

REGALEALI STEW *Meat with Vegetables in Broth*

*3 pounds boneless stew meat, such as beef, lamb, or veal, well trimmed and cut into 2- to
   3-inch pieces*
2 large onions, roughly chopped
4 waxy potatoes, peeled and cut into chunks
1 carrot, cut into chunks
2 stalks celery, cut into chunks
1 cup chopped, peeled, and seeded tomatoes
1 large eggplant, peeled and cut into chunks
2 medium zucchini, cut into chunks
8 cups stemmed and roughly chopped greens, such as Swiss chard, escarole, kale, cabbage
Salt
Black pepper
2 beef bouillon cubes

   Layer the ingredients in a large pot, starting with meat at the bottom and alternating vegetables and meat, ending with greens on top. Season each layer with salt and pepper to taste. Add the bouillon cubes and water to cover. Bring to a boil, reduce the heat, and cook, covered, until the meat is tender, about 1 1/2 to 2 hours. This serves 10 as a main course.

Another lamb stew we all like is *Spezzato di Montone alla Menta.* Serve it in a ring of *Purea di Patate.*

SPEZZATO DI MONTONE ALLA MENTA *Lamb Stew with Fresh Mint*

5 pounds lamb stew meat with bones or 3 pounds boneless shoulder or leg of lamb, well
trimmed and cut into 3- to 4-inch pieces
3 medium onions, sliced
3 beef bouillon cubes
3 to 4 cups water
Salt
Black pepper
1/2 cup mint leaves, chopped
1 cup white wine
1 tablespoon flour
Mint leaves, for garnish

Put the lamb and onions in a heavy pot and add the bouillon cubes and water to cover. Add salt and pepper to taste. Bring to a boil, reduce the heat, and simmer, uncovered, over medium-low heat for about 30 minutes. Add the chopped mint leaves and cook for 30 to 45 minutes more, until the lamb is tender enough to be cut with a fork and just begins to stick to the pan.

Remove the lamb from the pan and set it aside, keeping it warm. Discard the onions. Deglaze the pan with the wine. Use up to 1 cup of water with the flour to make a slurry. The amount of water you add depends on how much sauce you have and how thick it is. Stir the flour-water slurry into the pan and cook it over medium heat until the sauce thickens. Taste and correct the seasoning. Transfer the meat to a serving dish and spoon some sauce on top. Garnish with fresh mint leaves and serve immediately. Pass the remaining sauce in a sauceboat at the table. This serves 6 to 8 as a main course.

Fruits and Nuts

A quince tree stands in the middle of the garden. Its fragrant yellow fruit makes a stiff richly colored jelly, *Cotognata* (Quince Paste), which is very sweet and perfumed. We serve it with coffee, along with such other sweetmeats as *zuccata* and brittle.

My mother has great success with her *Cotognata*. The way she makes it is to cook quartered quinces with sliced lemons (about four pounds of quinces to two lemons) in a little water until soft. Then she purees the quinces in a food mill, weighs the puree, and adds an equal amount of sugar (by weight) and cooks the mixture in a nonreactive saucepan until it is very dense and comes away from the sides of the pan, like a pâte à choux. She packs the paste into lightly oiled molds—you could use a cake tin—and puts them, covered with cheesecloth, in a cool place for several days, until the paste feels dry. At that point, she removes the paste from the molds to let the top dry. When the paste is no longer sticky, she wraps it in wax paper. We all like *Cotognata* so much that she makes enough to last from one season to the next.

My mother makes another wonderful firm jelly, *Mostarda* (Wine Must Paste). This is really only for people who have their own winery. *Mostarda* is filled with the aroma of freshly crushed grapes; it reminds you of the *vendemmia* no matter what time of year it is.

We start picking walnuts in September. By then the green shell is almost off. The nuts are left out to dry, and soon the shell falls off completely, exposing the hard inner shell. Those fresh walnuts are a special treat. You have to pick off the bitter yellow skin before eating the kernel. It is so good! When the walnuts are completely dry, we make *Torrone di Noci*. Almond or pine nut brittle can be made following this recipe; substitute those nuts for the walnuts.

One year for my daughter Fabrizia's birthday, I made a cake covered with *Torrone di Noci*. We have called it *Torta di Fabrizia* (Fabrizia's Cake) ever since. It is *Pan di Spagna* (page 88), cut in half horizontally and filled with homemade jam. (Use whatever you have open; I prefer tangerine or grapefruit marmalade.) The cake is sprinkled with a rum syrup made especially for cakes and covered with crushed *Torrone di Noci*. Almond brittle is good, too.

TORRONE DI NOCI *Walnut Brittle*

¹/₂ cup sugar

¹/₂ cup honey

3 tablespoons freshly squeezed orange juice

2 cups walnut meats

Oil a clean, heat-resistant surface and the blade of a metal spatula with some vegetable oil.

Combine the sugar, honey, and orange juice in a small saucepan and cook over low heat without stirring. Shake the pan from time to time. When the sugar is almost melted, add the walnuts. Cook, stirring, for 3 to 4 minutes, until most of the foam subsides and the mixture becomes golden and thick. Pour the mixture out onto the prepared surface and spread it with the oiled spatula. Score it into 1¹/₂- to 2-inch pieces and, when it is cool enough to handle, break it into pieces along the score lines. Leave it to cool thoroughly. Keep the brittle in an airtight container. This makes about 1¹/₂ cups of brittle, which you can serve with coffee.

We don't grow our own chestnuts—the only chestnut tree we have marks the site of the dog cemetery. I don't know why, but we had great difficulty growing them. So we buy chestnuts in the fall when the nice big ones are in the shops, the ones that come from *oltre lo stretto* (across the Strait of Messina). We boil them or roast them in the fireplace and eat them while chatting or watching TV. To have them as dessert, we sometimes boil them and eat them out of the shell, cutting them in half with a knife first. If you are more sophisticated, like Costanza, you would cut a chestnut in two, put some butter on each half, and eat the nut from the shell with a teaspoon. We also cook shelled chestnuts with sugar; these are usually served with whipped cream.

Sweetened whole chestnuts are put up in jars for when we don't have time to make a dessert; they are like the first stage of marrons glacés. Dried chestnuts, called *crozzitelle* (small skulls), are also sold in the shops. You chew on these, but they are very hard.

There are a couple of pomegranate trees in my garden. The fruit, revered since ancient times, ripens at about the same time as the quince. Until recently I had eaten pomegranates only as a dessert, but I've started to use the seeds to garnish green salad. They add an excellent sweet-and-sour taste and a striking color.

We have persimmons in the garden, too. They are sweet, not tart like the ones that have known frost. I love their refreshing flavor. Persimmons are plentiful and cheap all over Sicily; everyone can afford to buy them. You see the very poorest people eating persimmons in the streets of the city.

The prickly pears are still good in the fall; we have red, yellow, and green ones. We peel away the thick prickly skin. The pits may seem daunting—just press them against the roof of your mouth with your tongue and swallow them whole. And figs are still around to be enjoyed.

Among the other table fruits we have at this time of year are the last of the peaches, yellow ones that are so hard and ugly you can only cut them up; nectarines; and little sweet plums that look and taste a bit like mirabelles. We also have some pears, through the wild trees that grace the countryside with their white blossoms in spring don't bear edible fruit.

We have started growing apples (Empires and Granny Smiths) with some degree of success, depending on the weather. They have to be picked at just the right moment. When they are fresh and have good texture, we include them in the fruit basket. Sometimes we bake them in red wine—*Mele al Regaleali Rosso*, we call them.

MELE AL REGALEALI ROSSO *Apples Baked in Regaleali Red Wine*

6 baking apples, cored
2 tablespoons freshly squeezed lemon juice
¹/₂ cup sugar
4 tablespoons raisins
2 tablespoons honey
3 cups Regaleali Rosso

Preheat the oven to 375°F.

Put the apples in a baking dish just large enough to hold them. Pour the lemon juice over the cored centers of the apples to prevent them from turning dark. Mix the sugar with the raisins and fill the apple cores. Spoon some honey on each apple and pour the wine over and around them.

Bake for 45 minutes to 1 hour, until the apples can be easily pierced with a fork and the tops are lightly browned. Remove the apples from the baking dish, set aside, and keep them warm. Boil down the wine sauce until thick and pour it back over the apples. Serve warm or at room temperature. This serves 6.

Perhaps because wine is so important at Regaleali, I tend to forget about table grapes. Our best table grape is the Zibibbo. In fact, some Sicilians won't even consider eating any other kind. The best Zibibbo grapes of all are believed to be the ones from the island of Pantelleria. They are big and juicy and very fragrant. We grow our own Zibibbo, but there is never enough.

I often pick ripe orange persimmons in the garden. My mother uses the yellow quince for her Cotognata (see page 175); Inzolia grapes are used for the Uva in Gelatina di Champagne (page 180). Pomegranates grow in abundance at Regaleali.

We also eat Inzolia grapes, which are grown for our white wine. They are refreshing when you go on a walk. When the grapes are golden and just ripe, the biggest and most beautiful clusters are hung the same way we hang cherry tomatoes and winter melons. We eat them as long as they last, usually until Christmastime.

One of the special desserts I make with grapes is *Uva in Gelatina di Champagne.* I love the way the champagne gelatin shimmers in the light. I gave the recipe to my daughter's mother-in-law, Giuppi Pietromarchi. At the time, her husband, Antonello, was Italian ambassador to The Hague. Their cook made it for a gala dinner and stuck long, thin candles in it. They told me it looked spectacular and that the queen of Holland asked Giuppi for the recipe.

UVA IN GELATINA DI CHAMPAGNE *Grapes in Champagne Gelatin*

2 envelopes unflavored gelatin
1³/₄ cups cold water
1¹/₃ cups sugar
Juice of 1 lemon, strained
1 bottle champagne
2 cups green grapes, peeled and seeded if necessary
Grapes and grape leaves, for garnish

Soften the gelatin in ¼ cup cold water, stirring to dissolve. Boil the remaining 1½ cups of water in a medium saucepan and add the sugar. Stir in the gelatin. Remove the pan from the heat and pour the liquid into a medium bowl. Stir in the lemon juice and the champagne.

Choose a good glass bowl for unmolding the dessert later. Pour about 1 cup of the gelatin mixture into the bottom and put the dish in the refrigerator so it will jell. Once this first layer has jelled, add another cup of liquid and return the dish to the refrigerator. Once this has jelled, scatter the grapes on the gelatin and cover with the rest of the liquid. Refrigerate until jelled. Unmold and serve garnished with grapes and grape leaves. This serves 6 to 8.

Wild Vegetables

I have been talking of fall according to the calendar, although in Sicily the season does not truly change until mid-October, when rain brings the long, hot, dry summer to a dramatic conclusion. For the next five months, Sicily is cool, even cold, and, especially, wet—if we are lucky. I say if we are lucky because in recent years it has not rained very much. In fact, in 1990 we had almost no rain, and everything was dying.

The rains in October and November can be heavy, filling the streambeds with raging torrents and often causing considerable damage. But they soak the parched soil, and the countryside turns miraculously green, overnight it seems. Salad greens, spinach, chard, cabbage, and broccoli take over the vegetable gardens. Wild vegetables begin to poke through the earth everywhere. Wild fennel, one of the two indispensable ingredients in *Pasta con le Sarde*, comes out and will grow until May. The wild greens are gathered and cooked. Various kinds are mixed together, blanched, and sautéed for a quick but delicious dish. The sautéed greens are often combined with pasta in *Pasta con la Verdura Amara*.

After a rain, the wild mushrooms come up in their secret places; only the shepherds know where. Wild mushrooms are rare in Sicily, but the cultivated ones in the shops are a good substitute. We don't even look at them, though, when the wild ones arrive. Then we prepare them *a spezzatino* (braised) to have with pasta or as a side dish for meat, or we grill the mushrooms over charcoal. We always preserve some in *Funghi all'Aceto sott'Olio*. You can do this with wild or cultivated "wild" mushrooms. Serve the preserved mushrooms as an appetizer or part of a picnic lunch.

FUNGHI ALL'ACETO SOTT'OLIO *Preserved Mushrooms*

2 pounds mushrooms, preferably wild

1/2 cup white wine vinegar

1 cup white wine

Salt

2 garlic cloves

3 small hot red peppers

4 cups olive oil

Clean the mushrooms and trim the stems. If you are using wild mushrooms, remove the stems if they are woody. Leave the mushrooms whole unless the caps are more than 3 inches in diameter. Cut larger mushrooms in pieces small enough to fit into the jars.

181

An old olive oil jar has been turned into a planter. Tonno sott' Olio is delicious with bread.

Pour the vinegar and wine into a 4- or 5-quart nonreactive saucepan, add salt to taste, garlic, and hot peppers and bring the mixture to a boil. Add the mushrooms and boil for about 3 minutes. Drain in a colander, squeezing the mushrooms lightly to extract the liquid. (Save the liquid if you are preparing more and reuse it.)

Pack the mushrooms tightly into sterilized jars, pushing down with your fingers or a spoon. Fill each jar with olive oil, making sure it surrounds and covers all the mushrooms and that there is no air left in the jar. Close the jars and store them in a cupboard for 2 months before using, so the mushrooms can absorb the flavors of the seasonings and the oil. This makes 2 pint jars.

‖ *Fish and Shellfish* ‖

Mario always puts up a large quantity of *Tonno sott'Olio* in fall, when he can get whole tuna weighing twenty-five to thirty pounds. We eat this straight from the jar with bread, or we add it to potato salad, where there are no other strong flavors to compete with it. For *Pasta con il Tonno in Bianco* and *Pasta con il Tonno Rosso*, though, we use store-bought canned tuna.

If you decide to preserve tuna, use only the white meat; the dark meat does not taste as good. And never let the fish come into contact with water that has not been boiled. Bacteria in the water—even otherwise harmless bacteria—would spoil the fish. Mario is adamant on this point.

TONNO SOTT'OLIO *Preserved Tuna*

2 pounds fresh tuna, preferably cut from the belly, neck, or tail in 1 piece, with the skin
6 bay leaves
2 to 3 cups olive oil

Bring a medium nonreactive saucepan of very well salted water to a boil. Add the tuna and the bay leaves, reduce the heat to a simmer, and cook for about 30 minutes. Remove the tuna from the heat and allow it to cool in the water for about 20 minutes.

Drain the tuna in a colander for 3 to 4 hours in a cool kitchen or in the refrigerator. Trim the skin and remove the cartilage and darker meat from the tuna, if necessary.

Pack the tuna into sterilized pint jars, leaving about 1 inch of space at the top. Add olive oil to cover. Let the jars rest for about 1 hour. Add additional oil to cover the tuna if necessary, being careful to allow at least ½ inch of space at the top of each jar.

Screw the lids on the jars and put them on a rack in a pot of cold water to cover. Boil for 30 minutes. Allow the jars to cool in the water overnight. Remove the jars, dry, and store in a dark cupboard for at least 3 months, to season, before eating. This makes 2 pint jars.

Bottarga (preserved tuna roe) is called *uovo di tonno* in Sicily. It is a great delicacy. The tuna roe is removed as soon as the fish is caught. It is pressed and salted, then left to dry in the sun. You have to be careful not to use too much of it; it is very salty.

When it is fresh and still pink inside, I like to crumble some on a piece of buttered homemade bread; this is the best way to eat it. For *Pasta con Uovo di Tonno* (Pasta with Preserved Tuna Roe), we sprinkle the grated *uovo di tonno* on top of *Pasta con il Tonno in Bianco*. We also sprinkle it on top of potato salad made with some homemade preserved tuna mixed in.

A more commonplace kind of preserved fish found all over Sicily, on tables rich and poor, is *sarde salate* (salted sardines). You see huge containers in the marketplace, and everyone keeps some of the fish on hand. In the old days, *sarde salate* were used to flavor pasta and bread, for a little goes a long way. Now they are more likely to be served as part of an antipasto or snack, rinsed and soaked in olive oil. I like them on top of a piece of thickly buttered bread.

A shellfish dish we often have in fall is *Cozze al Gratin*. The mussels are a real treat.

COZZE AL GRATIN *Mussels Gratin*

2 dozen mussels, bearded and scrubbed
¼ cup finely chopped onion
½ cup olive oil
½ cup fine breadcrumbs
1 tablespoon chopped parsley
Salt
Black pepper
Lemon wedges, for garnish

Place the mussels in a large sauté pan, cover, and place over high heat for about 3 minutes, shaking the pan. Remove any mussels that have opened. If some are still closed, return the pan to the heat for another minute. Remove all the opened mussels and discard any mussels that have not opened. Pull the mussels from the shells and place them in a bowl. Reserve 24 half shells—the best-looking ones.

Preheat the oven to 400°F.

Sauté the onion in ⅓ cup of the olive oil until golden, 2 to 3 minutes. Add the breadcrumbs, parsley, salt and pepper to taste, and a drop of oil. Mix in the mussels to coat them with the breadcrumb mixture. Put the mussels back into the reserved shells and place them in a baking dish. Sprinkle them with the remaining breadcrumb mixture. Drizzle with the remaining oil.

Bake the mussels for 10 minutes. Garnish with wedges of lemon. This serves 6 as a first course.

The Feast of San Martino

After the rains have transformed the landscape, Sicily enjoys a period of balmy weather—*l'estate di San Martino*, as Indian summer is called here and in most of Europe. The feast of San Martino, November 11, is the day to celebrate the end of the harvest and taste the new wine. San Martino is best known for sharing his cloak with a beggar, but he is also the patron saint of the harvest and of drinking and jovial gatherings. His day is always a time of great revelry, as workers from the vineyards, family, and friends arrive from all over. It is a holiday for everyone at Regaleali—it is the only day of the year the shepherds leave their flocks. As many as three hundred of us have gathered in the bottling room on occasion.

A banner proclaiming *"Pi San Martinu, ogni mostu e vinu"* ("By the feast of Saint Martin, the must has turned to wine," in Sicilian dialect) is pinned to an easel in the entrance. The cartons of wine bottles are moved out of the way, and tables are laid in the middle of the room, with a space left for the musicians and dancing. The room is decorated with vine branches—some green, some already turned red and gold—that were gathered at dawn. The guests are greeted by the music of a three-piece band with two singers, and during lunch anyone who feels like it can get up to sing or show off a few dance steps.

On this occasion, we drink rosé, the first wine to be ready. The menu is the same year after year: an antipasto of olives and cheese, *Anelletti alla Siciliana* for the pasta course, and barbecued lamb served with *Caponata di Melanzane* as the main course. Anelletti, a dense ring-shaped pasta, is unique to Sicily; lasagne or perciatelli can be substituted. We put fresh ricotta, drained and cut into pieces, on top. If you don't find good ricotta, you can use triangles of ricotta salata instead, but it won't be the same. Since Mario has the day off, the dessert comes from a bakery in Vallelunga, the village nearest to Regaleali.

When lunch is over, my father and mother get up to lead the dancing.

Breaded mussels ready to be gratineed (page 184). We like to garnish certain pasta dishes, like anelletti (opposite), with pieces of drained ricotta. It makes a very satisfying mouthful.

ANELLETTI ALLA SICILIANA *Anelletti Sicilian Style*

4 cups Maiale e Salsiccia al Ragù (page 188)

2 pounds anelletti or lasagne

1 cup grated pecorino or parmesan

1 1/2 pounds (3 cups) fresh ricotta, drained overnight, or 1/2 pound ricotta salata

Remove the meat (the pork and the sausage) from the ragù and chop it roughly. Reserve half the pork and sausage for the anelletti and reserve half for another meal. Pass the sauce through a food mill.

Cook the anelletti in boiling salted water until tender, about 25 minutes. Drain the pasta, and return it to the pan. Add half the sauce, mixing carefully.

Transfer half the pasta to a serving bowl. Put a ladleful of sauce, half of the chopped meat, and some grated pecorino on top. Add the remaining pasta, sauce, and meat. Garnish with pieces of ricotta or triangles of ricotta salata. Sprinkle with more pecorino. Serve immediately. This serves 10 as a pasta course.

Maiale e Salsiccia al Ragù *Pork and Sausage Ragù*

2 pounds pork butt or boneless shoulder, in 1 piece

1 cup olive oil

1/2 cup red wine

4 cups water

2 large onions, finely chopped

4 garlic cloves, minced

2 tablespoons Estratto di Pomodoro (see page 115) or 6 tablespoons sun-dried tomato paste

4 cups Salsa di Pomodoro Passata (page 114)

6 fresh bay leaves

2 to 3 tablespoons sugar

Ground hot pepper (optional)

Salt

Black pepper

1 pound Italian sausage

Dry the pork with paper towels. Pour about half of the oil into a heavy skillet and brown the pork evenly and well. Sprinkle the wine over the browned meat and loosen all the bits on the bottom of the pan. Add 3 cups of the water and set aside.

Pour the remaining oil into a deep, heavy pot, large enough to hold all the ingredients. Add the onions and garlic and sauté until they are just beginning to color. Dissolve the estratto in the remaining 1 cup of water and stir it into the pot. Pour in the salsa and add the bay leaves. Add sugar to taste and hot pepper, if desired. Season to taste with salt and pepper. Add the browned pork and all the liquid.

Cover the sauce and simmer, stirring occasionally, for 1 1/2 hours, until thickened and reduced. Remove the sausage from the casings and crumble it into the sauce. Cook for 30 minutes, until the sausage has lost all its pink color. This makes about 2 quarts of sauce.

Cheese

Cheese making, which is suspended at the end of June, begins again in November on the feast of San Martino and continues through the winter and spring. The first ricotta of the season is not considered to be very fine. It is far better in winter and springtime, when the pastures are more lush.

Once the lambs that were born at the end of August have been weaned, the ewes are milked twice a day. They are brought to the sheepfold, and one by one they are pushed up to the gate for milking. *Testa rossa* sheep are good milkers, but the shepherds still encourage the ewes to give more.

The milk is transported immediately in airtight stainless-steel milk cans to the dairy, where Toto Di Martino, head shepherd like his father before him, makes the cheese every morning and evening, except on his day off. Then one of the other shepherds makes it, but none is as good as Toto's.

The way Toto makes the cheese has hardly changed since the days of the ancient Greeks. He starts by pouring the still-warm milk into a large chestnut-wood vat and adding natural rennet, derived from the stomach lining of milk-fed lambs. The interior of this vessel has turned dark over the years from the milk and the heat. When the milk has clabbered, in about two hours, Toto pours in hot water, breaks up the curds with a long-handled wooden stirrer called *la ruotola*, and pours the mixture into a rush basket set in a bucket to catch the whey. He transfers the curds from the basket to a *madia*, a large wooden box with sloping sides, which is tilted so the curds can drain farther, and presses and squeezes out as much of the whey as he can. Then he cuts the curds, which will become fresh *tuma* (curd cheese), into blocks and packs them into another basket to continue to drain.

Fresh *tuma* is soft and creamy and has a very pleasant taste. We eat it plain with salt and pepper and in salad with tomatoes, the way one would use mozzarella. We also put slices on top of dishes we want to bake, like *Broccoli con Olive Nere* or *Uova a Trippa*, and on pizza.

The *tuma* is salted after about three days—"when it begins to stink," Toto says—then every eight days or so it is massaged evenly with the salt and juices that come out of the cheese. Then it is left until someone decides to cut the cheese and eat it. This *primo sale* has a sharp but still delicate flavor.

After about six months of salting, *primo sale* becomes pecorino. The cheese is usually a wheel about five inches high and six or seven inches across. (Toto makes some smaller ones every year for me to put in the Christmas baskets I give my friends.) Each one is imprinted with the pattern of the basket in which it was made. It tastes wonderful with a glass of Rosso del Conte, but you can also grate it to put on pasta.

The pastoral life. A newborn lamb is followed anxiously by its mother; the other ewes wait their turn to be milked.

We always make a few cheeses with peppercorns or with coriander seeds, two traditional flavorings, for those who like cheese with something in it. My mother enjoys experimenting with flavors; she asks Toto to put in anything reasonable, herbs or saffron, for example. All these are added when the *tuma* is put into the basket. As usual, some of us like one more than the other, but it is always fun to try them.

While Toto forms the *tuma* from the curds, the whey is poured into a large tinned copper caldron, which is set over a lively fire of dry vine or olive branches, to make ricotta. Once the whey nears a boil, it is stirred constantly with a fig-wood stick. At the same time it is skimmed constantly to remove lime and any impurities that rise to the surface. It is quite a sight to see Toto with the wooden stick in one hand and the metal ladle in the other, turning them in opposite directions. After about an hour, the ricotta rises to the surface. It is removed with a perforated ladle and set to drain in baskets. These used to be woven of rush by the shepherds, but now most are plastic. We still use the traditional rush baskets for the *primo sale* (young pecorino) and pecorino, though.

The first ricotta to come to the surface is the very best, and we eat it just as it is or seasoned with salt. I love this *ricotta calda* (warm ricotta). It is so full of flavor.

Homemade fresh ricotta is a luxury to be enjoyed only by those who live in the country—and, sad to say, not much longer for them, either. Young people are not interested in pursuing the pastoral way of life, spending their days with the flock in the pastures and milking the ewes at dawn and dusk. Nowadays, too, the trend is to send the milk off to an industrial dairy rather than make the cheese on the farm.

Ricotta is one of the essential ingredients of Sicilian cuisine; it is always on the table. We eat it warm on its own, or with spinach or bitter greens. We put it on pasta and in frittatas. We often have it as a dessert, sweetened with honey or jam. Now that I make my own marmalades, we serve the ricotta with tangerine marmalade; people just love it. We also use it as a sweet cream in pastries. If you ever find ewe's milk ricotta, be sure to buy a lot and freeze it. It won't be as good as the fresh, but it will be better than commercial ricotta.

You can doctor cow's milk ricotta with ricotta salata for your *Torta di Ricotta con Canditi*. When Mario makes it, he serves hot *Crema di Cioccolata* or strawberry or sour-cherry syrup with the cake, but that may be a case of gilding the lily.

TORTA DI RICOTTA CON CANDITI
Ricotta Cheesecake with Candied Fruit

2 pounds ricotta, preferably skim milk

1/4 cup fine breadcrumbs

1/2 pound ricotta salata, crumbled

1 1/2 cups sugar

7 large eggs

Grated peel of 1 orange

1/2 cup semisweet chocolate chips

1/4 cup shelled unsalted pistachios

1/2 cup pine nuts

1/2 cup golden raisins

1/2 cup candied fruit, chopped

2 teaspoons flour

Salt

Put the ricotta in a colander; place the colander in a bowl, and allow the cheese to drain in the refrigerator for at least 1 hour but preferably overnight.

Preheat the oven to 325°F. Generously butter an 8- or 9-inch springform pan. Sprinkle it with the breadcrumbs.

Mix the ricotta, ricotta salata, sugar, and eggs in a bowl. Pass the mixture twice through a food mill or process in a food processor. Dredge the grated orange peel, chocolate chips, pistachios, pine nuts, raisins, and candied fruit in the flour with a pinch of salt. Add these to the cheese mixture.

Pour the ricotta mixture into the prepared pan and bake 1 to 1 1/2 hours, until lightly golden. The center should feel slightly firm, and the cake will begin to crack in the middle. Turn off the oven and leave the cake in it to dry for 10 to 20 minutes, or until the oven is cool. When the cheesecake is cool, remove it from the pan and serve. This serves 8 to 10.

Testa rossa sheep are good milkers. Toto separates the clabbered milk into curds and whey. Ricotta is skimmed from the boiling whey and transferred to plastic baskets. Toto packs the curds down into a rush basket.

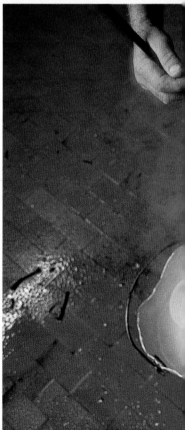

For savory dishes, you can mix the ricotta with a little goat cheese rather than ricotta salata. Try this for *Pasta con la Ricotta in Bianco.* You might think the dish would be too bland, but if you use the flavored ricotta and a good pecorino, it won't be. A good dish to follow this is *Castrato al Rosso del Conte* with mushrooms and little onions.

PASTA CON LA RICOTTA IN BIANCO
Pasta with Ricotta and Pecorino

$^1/_2$ *pound ricotta*
$^1/_4$ *pound goat cheese*
2 tablespoons butter, softened
$^1/_2$ *cup grated pecorino*
Salt
Black pepper
1 pound spaghetti
Grated pecorino, for garnish

Mix the ricotta and goat cheese together in the bowl you will use to serve the spaghetti. Add the butter and pecorino. Season generously with salt and pepper. Place the bowl in a warm place while you cook the spaghetti.

Cook the spaghetti in boiling salted water until al dente. When the spaghetti is almost done, remove 1 cup of the cooking water. Use as much of it as you need to thin the sauce. Drain the spaghetti, pour it into the bowl, and toss with the sauce. Sprinkle with some pecorino and serve immediately. Pass additional pecorino at the table. This serves 4 as a pasta course.

CASTRATO AL ROSSO DEL CONTE *Lamb Stew Rosso del Conte*

3 pounds boneless leg of lamb, cut into large pieces
1 medium onion, sliced
2 bay leaves
1 bottle Rosso del Conte
¹/₄ cup plus 1 tablespoon olive oil
1 cup brandy
Salt
Black pepper
2 pounds white mushrooms, sliced
¹/₂ pound pancetta, cut into ¹/₂-inch dice
2 pounds whole pearl onions, peeled
3 tablespoons butter
1 tablespoon sugar
2 tablespoons flour, mixed with ¹/₂ cup water

Combine the lamb with the onion and bay leaves in a glass bowl and pour in enough red wine to cover. Marinate in the refrigerator overnight. Drain the lamb pieces, reserving the marinade, and dry them with paper towels. Heat ¹/₄ cup olive oil in a sauté pan and brown the lamb lightly. When the pieces have colored and the juices have evaporated, add the brandy. Ignite and let the brandy burn until evaporated.

Place the meat in a heavy saucepan, add the reserved marinade, and salt and pepper to taste. Cover and cook slowly over low heat for about 1¹/₂ hours, or until the meat is tender. The sauce should just cover the meat; add additional wine if it's needed.

While the meat is cooking, sauté the mushrooms and pancetta in 1 tablespoon olive oil until lightly colored. In a separate saucepan, sauté the pearl onions briefly in the butter. Add the sugar and enough water to cover, and simmer, uncovered, until all the water is absorbed. When the meat is done, add the mushroom-pancetta mixture and the onions. Simmer for a few minutes. Add the flour-water slurry and bring the mixture to a boil, cooking over low heat until the sauce is slightly thickened. Correct the seasonings if necessary. This serves 8 to 10 as a main course.

One dish that is absolutely unforgettable when Mario makes it with our ricotta is *Guastelle* (Spleen Sandwiches). *Guastella* is actually the name for a certain kind of soft roll with sesame seeds on top; it resembles a hamburger bun. You cut it in half and fill it with warmed ricotta, caciocavallo, and beef spleen, an organ meat that is much appreciated in Sicily. The spleen is sliced and cooked literally swimming in lard. Since spleen is not available in the United States, you will have to have *schiette* (spinster) *guastelle*, as we say at Regaleali. *Maritate* (married) would be with spleen. (Elsewhere in Sicily, these terms refer to the absence or presence of ricotta.) *Guastelle* are really street food, and there is a *focacceria* in the Piazza San Francesco in Palermo where they still make them.

Another street food that we enjoy at home is *Sfincione*. We use *tuma*, but you can substitute mozzarella. Sometimes we make a *pizza del caseificio* (cheese pizza) with all our own special cheeses—*tuma, primo sale,* and pecorino. When I make *Sfincione*, I use our cheeses, but you can substitute other mild melting cheeses, as Mario does.

When he makes *Sfincione*, he usually prepares a big batch of dough and divides it in two. He prepares one with the cheese; the other he tops with chunky tomatoes, either fresh or canned, instead of the breadcrumb mixture, and he sprinkles the tomatoes liberally with oregano. It isn't necessary to drizzle as much oil over the tomatoes as over the breadcrumb-and-cheese topping, since the juice of the tomatoes keeps the pizza moist.

SFINCIONE *Sicilian Pizza*

2 *medium onions, sliced*

³/₄ *cup olive oil*

Pasta di Sfincione

2 *cups all-purpose flour*

1 *cup semolina flour*

1 *teaspoon salt*

1 *cake compressed yeast or 1 package dry yeast*

1 *cup warm water*

1 *egg*

2 *tablespoons butter, cut into* ¹/₄*-inch dice*

↩

4 *anchovy fillets, cut into 4 pieces*

³/₄ *pound fresh mozzarella, sliced*

¹/₄ *pound Emmentaler, julienned*

¹/₄ *pound Gouda, julienned*

¹/₂ *cup grated parmesan*

¹/₄ *cup grated caciocavallo or pecorino*

2 *to 3 tablespoons dried oregano*

³/₄ *cup breadcrumbs*

Guastelle sandwiches are much appreciated in Sicily.

Sauté the onions in ¹/₂ cup of the olive oil over medium heat until golden, 15 to 20 minutes. Remove the onions from the heat and set aside.

Measure the all-purpose and semolina flours into a bowl and add the salt. Make a well in the center; add the yeast, water, egg, and butter. Work the dough until it forms a ball and turn it out onto a work surface. The dough will be wet initially but will become smooth after you work it for 3 to 4 minutes. Continue to knead the dough for 10 to 15 minutes, until it is smooth and elastic.

Oil a 9×12-inch baking sheet. Roll out the dough and shape it to fit the pan. Place the anchovy pieces on the dough in rows, cover with the mozzarella, sprinkle with the Emmentaler and Gouda, and spread the onions on top. Mix the parmesan and caciocavallo together and spread over the onions. Sprinkle with oregano. Spread the breadcrumbs evenly on top. Press all the ingredients into the dough, using the palms of your hands. Drizzle the remaining olive oil on top and cover with a kitchen towel. Place in a warm spot and allow it to rise until double, about 45 minutes.

Preheat the oven to 400°F.

Bake the Sfincione until the crust is browned underneath and the cheese has melted, about 40 to 50 minutes. Let it stand for 15 minutes, then cut it into squares and serve. This serves 12 as a snack or 6 as a first course.

If you like the taste of pizza, you can use the same ingredients—sliced onions, tomatoes, and oregano—with potatoes. *Patate a Sfincione* are served as a main course.

PATATE A SFINCIONE *Potatoes Pizza Style*

1 large onion, sliced
2 pounds boiling potatoes
1¹/₂ cups Salsa Pic-Pac (page 110)
1 tablespoon dried oregano
¹/₂ cup grated caciocavallo
¹/₂ cup olive oil

Put the onion in salted cold water to soak. Boil the potatoes in well-salted water until just done. Peel and slice. Drain the onion.

Preheat the oven to 375°F. Lightly oil an 8×12-inch baking dish.

Spread a third of the potatoes on the bottom of the dish, cover with a third of the onion slices, salsa, and oregano. Sprinkle with cheese and drizzle with oil. Repeat twice. Bake the potatoes for 20 minutes. Let them stand for at least 10 minutes before serving. This serves 4 as a main dish.

We seldom buy cheese, since we all prefer those Toto makes. One we do buy is caciocavallo, a cow's milk cheese, especially for *Formaggio all'Argentiera*. If you can't find good caciocavallo, you can substitute good Asiago and provolone.

This is a dish that everyone likes because it is so tasty and easy. The story told about it is that a poor silversmith invented it to trick his neighbors into thinking he was rich enough to eat meat. When they smelled the heavenly aromas wafting from his kitchen, they were indeed fooled, and they copied the dish and named it after him.

Rule one about this dish: Make sure everyone is in the kitchen and ready to eat before starting. Rule two: Expect to burn your tongue.

FORMAGGIO ALL'ARGENTIERA *Silversmith's Cheese*

¹/₃ cup olive oil
1¹/₂ pounds caciocavallo or ³/₄ pound Asiago and ³/₄ pound provolone,
*   sliced ¹/₄ inch thick*
1 to 2 tablespoons dried oregano
1 to 2 tablespoons red wine vinegar
Italian country bread, cut into chunks

Pour the oil into a 10-inch skillet and cover with slices of cheese. Sprinkle with oregano. Heat the cheese over medium heat until it starts to melt. Turn, pour on the vinegar, and remove it from the heat. Eat immediately, dipping thick chunks of Italian country bread into the pan. This appetizer or snack serves 4 if you are very hungry or 6 if you are not.

At the other end of the formality scale from *Formaggio all'Argentiera* is the dish we call *Sformato di Formaggio Principe di Galles*, so named because we served it when the Prince of Wales came to visit Regaleali, and he raved about it. We usually serve the *sformato* as a first dish. You can eat only a thin slice, since it's so rich, even though the pastry is incredibly light. When I asked Mario how he gets it that way, he answered, "The dough tells me when it's ready."

SFORMATO DI FORMAGGIO PRINCIPE DI GALLES
Prince of Wales Cheese Brioche

Pasta per Brioche

8 cups flour

3 cakes compressed yeast or 3 packages dry yeast

1 cup warm water

1 1/2 teaspoons salt

8 egg yolks, at room temperature

1 egg

1/2 pound butter, softened

1/4 cup milk (optional)

Ripieno di Formaggi

1/2 cup cubed Fontina

1/2 cup cubed Gruyère

1/2 cup cubed Edam

1/2 cup cubed Gouda

1/3 cup cooked peas

1/2 cup cubed boiled ham

↤

2 egg whites beaten with 2 teaspoons water, for egg wash

Pour the flour onto a work surface or into a bowl and form a well in the center. Dissolve the yeast in the water, add the salt, and pour this into the well. Add all the egg yolks, the egg, and the butter. Mix together gently to form a dough. Knead the dough on a floured surface until it is smooth and easily forms a ball and no longer sticks to your hands, about 20 minutes. If the dough is too stiff, add the milk, little by little, while kneading. Cover the dough with a clean kitchen towel and set aside to rest.

Grease and lightly flour a 10-inch springform pan. Line the bottom with parchment paper or aluminum foil.

Cut the dough into 2 pieces, one slightly larger than the other. Roll out the larger piece of dough into a circle 4 to 5 inches larger than the base of the pan. Lift the dough into the pan and press gently into the bottom and sides of the pan. Allow the dough to hang over the sides of the pan.

Fill the dough shell by making layers of the cheeses, peas, and ham. Roll the remaining dough into a circle slightly larger than the pan and place it on top of the filling. Trim the edges of the bottom dough to a 1-inch border. Fold the overhanging dough up and over and pinch the edges together to seal. Cover with a clean kitchen towel and allow to rise until doubled, 1 to 1 1/2 hours.

Preheat the oven to 400°F.

Brush the dough with the egg wash. Bake for 1 hour, until golden brown. Let the sformato cool to room temperature before serving so the cheese will set. This is a very rich first course and will serve about 16.

Timbaletti are little timbales, usually made in the kind of molds you would use for *baba au rhum.* The pasta shells are filled with a tomato-and-meat sauce, then breaded and fried. They also can be baked. *Timbaletti* are served on their own as a first course or included in a *Fritto Misto.*

TIMBALETTI *Filled Pasta Timbales*

Béchamel
  3 tablespoons butter
  4 tablespoons flour
  1 cup milk
  ❧
  1 1/2 cups Ragoncino (page 134), with 1/2 pound Italian sausage, casing removed, fried
    with the ground beef
  1/2 pound capellini
  1 1/2 to 2 cups flour
  3 eggs, beaten with 3 teaspoons water
  1 1/2 to 2 cups fine breadcrumbs
  Oil, for frying

Timbaletti, filled with ragoncino and ready to fry.

Make a béchamel by melting the butter in a medium saucepan. Remove it from the heat, and whisk in the flour. Gradually whisk in the milk, return the sauce to the heat, and cook, stirring constantly, until thickened, about 20 minutes. Set aside.

Butter 20 timbaletti molds and set out next to a bowl of ice water and the ragoncino.

Cook the capellini in boiling salted water until less than al dente. Drain the pasta and mix it with the béchamel.

Fill the timbaletti molds with the pasta mixture, dipping your thumb in the ice water and pushing it into the center of each of the Timbaletti to form a walnut-sized indentation. Fill each with about 1 tablespoon of ragoncino and cover with more pasta. Turn the mold over and push it down on the counter, using a twist of your wrist to cut the edges. Continue doing this until all the molds are filled. Set the filled molds aside for at least 1 hour. Refrigerate or freeze any leftover ragoncino and use it as a sauce for pasta or as a filling for vegetables.

Put the flour, eggs, and breadcrumbs in 3 separate bowls. Carefully remove each of the Timbaletti from its mold and dip it in the flour, then the egg, then the breadcrumbs.

Preheat 3 inches of oil in a deep fryer to 325°F. The oil should sizzle when tested with the edge of one of the Timbaletti. Deep-fry the Timbaletti until golden. Drain them on paper towels and serve hot. This makes 20, which will serve 10 people as a first course, more as part of a Fritto Misto.

Another elaborate first dish we make is *Timballo di Capellini,* a sturdy pasta shell filled with ham and melting cheeses. Another filling we often use is *ragoncino.* If you want, you can make the crust with rice or mashed potatoes; I like all three.

TIMBALLO DI CAPELLINI *Timbale with a Pasta Crust*

Béchamel

2 1/2 *cups milk*

1 beef bouillon cube

1 tablespoon butter

1 tablespoon flour

Salt

Black pepper

֍

1/2 *cup breadcrumbs*

1 pound capellini

1/2 *cup chopped boiled ham*

1/2 *cup cubed Fontina*

1/2 *cup cubed Emmentaler*

3/4 *cup grated parmesan*

2 tablespoons butter

Start the béchamel by pouring the milk into a small saucepan. Add the bouillon cube and heat the milk, stirring to dissolve the bouillon cube. Melt the butter in a saucepan. Remove from the heat and whisk in the flour. Whisk the warm milk into the flour. Return to the heat and cook, stirring constantly, until thickened, about 20 minutes. Season to taste with salt and pepper. Set aside.

Preheat the oven to 350°F. Butter a 12-inch springform pan. Dust the bottom and sides of the pan with some of the breadcrumbs and shake off the excess.

Cook the capellini in boiling salted water until less than al dente. Drain the pasta and toss it rapidly with 2 cups of the béchamel. In a separate bowl, combine the remaining béchamel with the ham and cheeses and set aside.

Line the bottom and sides of the springform pan with three-fourths of the capellini-béchamel mixture to form a shell for the filling. If the capellini sticks to your fingers while you are shaping it, wet your hands and continue. Fill the shell with the ham-cheese-béchamel mixture. Cover with the remaining capellini, pressing down lightly. Dot with the butter and sprinkle with the remaining breadcrumbs.

Bake until the crust is golden, about 50 minutes to 1 hour. Let the timballo rest for at least 15 minutes. Remove it from the pan, transfer it to a serving plate, and serve it warm. This serves 8 as a first course.

The Feast of Santa Lucìa

Santa Lucìa is the patron saint of vision and after the Virgin Mary the most venerated saint in Italy. In the old Julian calendar, the feast of Santa Lucìa was celebrated on the shortest, darkest day of the year, the first day of winter. In the Gregorian calendar, her feast day falls on December 13.

Santa Lucìa is honored in a very special way in Sicily: no food made from milled wheat is supposed to be eaten on her day. That does not mean it is a day of fasting—far from it! Potatoes, *Panelle*, which are made from chick-pea flour, and *Cuccìa* (Saint Lucy's Pudding), made from wheat berries, are all consumed in great quantities.

Abstaining from milled wheat commemorates one of Santa Lucìa's most famous miracles. Sicily was afflicted by a grave famine one year when the grain crop failed. Then, according to legend, a ship laden with wheat docked in Palermo on her feast day and saved the people from starvation. They boarded the ship and took the grain and cooked it without grinding it.

In the course of time, that simple bowl of boiled wheat has become quite an elaborate dessert. Cooked wheat berries are mixed with either freshly made *Biancomangiare* or ricotta sweetened with sugar or honey and with some chopped *zuccata* or candied fruit stirred in. Some people flavor their *Cuccìa* with *Vino Cotto* (Cooked Wine), an ancient sweetener made by boiling down clear unfermented wine must.

At Regaleali, we do not strictly follow the Santa Lucìa traditions. We serve both pasta and potatoes, both bread and *Panelle*. We make our *Cuccìa* rich with ricotta cheese. That way, nobody goes away disappointed.

L'Inverno

WINTER

The winter sunshine in Sicily is

one of the most beautiful things you can experience. I remember one

magical day, one of those days I call a gift from God. The sky

was blue, blue, blue, and the countryside green everywhere. From where I

stood, I could see the Madonie Mountains, covered with snow,

and Etna, also snowcapped, in the distance. All around me was silence,

except for a few birds here and there talking to one another.

WINTER CAN BE WARM in the sun, but much of the time it is cloudy and cold. The *tramontana*, the wind that blows from the north, feels like ice, and even the scirocco, the wind from the south, is cold in winter. There are still cauliflower and kohlrabi in the garden, but not much else. The fields are bare, and though the grass is green, it stays short. The trees are without leaves, except for the evergreen olive and the citrus trees. In the vineyards, the canes of the pruned vines wave in the wind.

Wine

In the cellar and storage rooms the wines are aging in their barrels and bottles. Everyone is dreaming about what to do next.

One year my brother, Lucio, decided after great doubts and uncertainty to change the labels and bottles to give the wine a new look. My friend Sandra Ducrot had done the sketch of the label for the Regaleali Rosso, Bianco, and Rosato wines in 1966. It was the only label for a long time, and it was the first image with which Regaleali wine became famous. Sandra now lives in Paris, far away from me, but I think of her every day when I see her drawing and even when I don't see it.

When Lucio got this idea, he hired some graphic designers to create new labels, but my father sent them packing. He liked to design the labels himself. He used to lock himself in his studio and, after consulting with various family members and friends and shouting a lot at everyone, would come up with something quite unexpected, often shocking, but always effective.

The label of the Nozze d'Oro, for example, features a photograph of my parents in profile. My sister Costanza was taking photographs for weeks. I didn't envy her. She

My sister Costanza. My father and mother in Papa's study; photo albums dating back to their courtship fill the shelves, and drawings cover the walls.

must have taken hundreds of photos. In one there was too much nose, in another too much chin. Then there was the question of glasses: which was better, with or without? Not to mention that some people were not happy to have their parents' picture pasted on a bottle. But the label turned out to be charming.

The label for our sparkling wines has art nouveau lettering that emphasizes the brilliant colors of a stylized peacock. The inspiration came from a stained-glass window done in 1929 by Bevilacqua that is installed over the front door of my parents' summer home in Mondello, near Palermo.

The first label my father had nothing to do with is the one for the Villa Tasca white wine. He had designed a beautiful label that represented the Villa Tasca in Palermo, showing the lake, the swans, the gate, and the front of the house. But it was considered too imposing for the fresh and modern wine it was to represent, and the designers were brought in. They did something similar but more of a sketch, lightly colored, which was considered more appropriate.

Lucio had the idea for the Chardonnay label. It is in quite a different mode from the others, more austere, matte black with the family crest in blue and gold and just the two words "Chardonnay" and "Regaleali" printed on it. The Cabernet Sauvignon is in the same style.

‖ *Snowfall* ‖

Sometimes it snows at Regaleali, but the snow rarely stays. The longest that I remember it staying was in 1981. It was New Year's Eve, and Costanza, her husband, Paolo, and I had decided at the last minute to go, unannounced, to Regaleali to wish my parents a happy New Year. Rain mixed with snow started to fall, and Costanza and I were pulling Paolo's leg, saying he wouldn't be able to get back to Palermo the next day. My parents were quite surprised to see us. They were alone, and the five of us had a wonderful dinner together.

The next morning when I woke up, it was eerie. There was no noise at all outside—no tractors, no cars, no rain, no wind. I got up and looked out the window. Everything was covered with snow, a lot of snow. The snow on the branches of the pomegranate trees— and the quince and the olive—looked like lace. It took Paolo three days to get back to town, but Costanza and I stayed with our parents. What a nice visit we had!

The two of us and our mother had a great time in the kitchen. One day Costanza made her famous *Minestra di Fagioli*. Another day our mother made *Minestra di Lenticchie*. She and Costanza really rule the soup kettle. They throw everything in without measuring, cook it for a while, and ladle out something heavenly.

MINESTRA DI FAGIOLI *Cranberry Bean Soup*

1 pound dried cranberry beans
1 large onion, cut into chunks
1 stalk celery, cut into chunks
2 carrots, cut into chunks
1/4 pound pancetta, chopped
2 garlic cloves, minced
2 cups peeled, seeded, and chopped tomatoes
1/2 cup chopped parsley
1/4 pound spaghetti or tagliatelle, broken up and cooked al dente
Salt
Black pepper
1 garlic clove, minced, for garnish
Olive oil, for garnish

Soak the beans in cold water to cover overnight. Drain and place them in a large saucepan with the onion, celery, and carrots. Cover with water, bring to a boil, lower the heat, and simmer until the beans are almost done, about 1 hour.

Meanwhile, sauté the pancetta until it renders its fat. Add the garlic cloves and sauté. Add the tomatoes and parsley and cook for 15 minutes.

Remove 2 cups of beans from the saucepan and puree them in a food mill or food processor. Stir the puree back into the soup. Add the tomato mixture and the spaghetti to the soup. Taste and season with salt and pepper. Cook the soup to warm it through. Garnish with minced garlic and a stream of olive oil. This soup serves 8 as a first course.

MINESTRA DI LENTICCHIE *Lentil Soup*

1 pound lentils, soaked in cold water to cover overnight
1 medium onion, cut into chunks
1 stalk celery, cut into chunks
1 carrot, cut into chunks
6 cups water
1 chicken or beef bouillon cube
Salt
Black pepper
Olive oil, for garnish

Drain the lentils and put them and the vegetables into a large saucepan. Add the water and the bouillon cube and bring the soup to a boil. Reduce the heat and cook until the lentils are done, about 45 minutes. Taste and season with salt and pepper. Serve warm with a drizzle of olive oil. This serves 4 to 6 as a first course.

For lunch that snowbound day I made *Frittatine di Pasta*, one of our favorite dishes from childhood. Most of the time these pasta cakes are made with leftover pasta, but we didn't have enough, so I cooked up a batch of capellini expressly to fry it. It's amazing that such a simple dish can be so good. When you make it, be sure to use a nonstick pan; otherwise the cheese will stick to the bottom, and you'll never get the pasta out.

FRITTATINE DI PASTA *Fried Pasta Cakes*

³/₄ pound capellini
3 tablespoons butter
Olive oil, for frying
¹/₃ to ¹/₂ cup grated caciocavallo or parmesan

Cook the capellini in boiling salted water until less than al dente. Drain and put it into a medium bowl. Toss with the butter to coat. Measure out 6 portions in shallow soup dishes, forming the capellini into 5- or 6-inch cakes. Stack the dishes, putting an empty one on top, and weight them down with a can to flatten the pasta cakes. Set aside to cool.

Choose a small nonstick pan about the same size as the pasta cakes, and place it over moderate heat. Add 1 teaspoon of olive oil and spread it around with a piece of paper towel to coat the pan evenly. Sprinkle the bottom of the pan with about

1 tablespoon of cheese. When the cheese starts to melt, slip a pasta cake into the pan and cook about 4 to 5 minutes over medium heat, pushing any extra cheese toward the cake. Lift the cake around the edges and when it's brown on the bottom, slide it out onto a plate. Wipe the bottom of the pan with a bit more oil and sprinkle it with more cheese. When it melts, return the pasta to the pan, cooking the other side. Shake the pan to keep it from sticking. Remove the pasta from the pan and set it aside in a warm place until all the frittatine are done. Serve warm. This makes enough frittatine to serve 6 as a pasta course.

We didn't just eat comfort food, though. One night, Mario made *Pollo Conti d'Almerita*, a wonderful dish of chicken with champagne and heavy cream. It is surprisingly light and delicate, and you can taste the French background behind *monzù* cooking. Normally we would have this dish with rice formed into a ring, but this time we had it with *Patate a Spezzatino*.

POLLO CONTI D'ALMERITA *Chicken in Champagne Sauce*

One 2- to 3-pound chicken
¼ cup olive oil
Salt
Black pepper
1 red onion, minced
1 bottle Regaleali champagne
1 cup water
½ cup heavy cream
1 heaping tablespoon flour, mixed with ½ cup water

Brown the chicken in the olive oil in a sauté pan over medium heat. Season to taste with salt and pepper. Add the onion and continue cooking. After 15 minutes, add ½ cup of the champagne. Cook for 15 minutes, then add an additional ½ cup of champagne and the water. Cook until tender, about 45 minutes to 1 hour in all.

Take the chicken from the pan, remove and discard the skin, and cut the chicken into 4 to 6 pieces. Set the chicken aside and keep it warm. Degrease the sauce and puree it. Return the puree to the pan, add the remaining champagne and the cream, and whisk together. Adjust the seasonings. Whisk in the flour-water slurry and cook until the sauce is thickened. Arrange the chicken on a serving platter and cover it with some of the sauce. Pour the rest of the sauce into a sauceboat to pass at the table. Serve warm. This serves 4 as a main course.

PATATE A SPEZZATINO *Braised Potatoes*

1 small onion, chopped
2 garlic cloves, minced
¹/₄ cup olive oil
4 cups peeled and cubed potatoes
2 cups water
¹/₂ cup chopped parsley
Salt
Black pepper

Sauté the onion and garlic in the olive oil in a large sauté pan for 2 to 3 minutes, just until golden. Add the potatoes and the water and cook, covered, for about 20 minutes, until the potatoes are softened. Uncover, add the parsley, and stir for about 5 minutes, until the potatoes are partially mashed. Season the potatoes to taste with salt and pepper, and serve them warm. This serves 4 as a side dish.

‖ *Citrus* ‖

Citrus is grown extensively in eastern Sicily, with citrus groves even around the slopes of Mount Etna. In the western part of the island, every landowner has a grove or at least a couple of citrus trees in the garden. The perfume of the trees in bloom fills the Sicilian air late at night. The honey from those blossoms is the most delicious on earth.

Besides the familiar kinds of grapefruit, orange, tangerine, and lemon, some of the old varieties are still grown in Sicily. We have the very sweet, perfumed *arancio vaniglia* (vanilla orange), which is my favorite; the *arancio amaro* (the bitter, or Seville, orange); the *limone dolce* (sweet lemon); and the *lumia*, which looks like a round lemon but has a sweet taste. The *lumia* is known especially for its fragrance. We also have so-called Brazilian oranges (navels) and Portugal oranges (juice oranges), blood oranges, clementines, and citrons.

Some years our grapefruit is juicy, others not; it depends on the rains. It is hard to believe that this popular fruit was not appreciated until fairly recently. Fulco Cerda della Verdura, the world-famous jewelry designer known as Fulco, who was a great friend of my in-laws, grew up in a villa near Palermo. In his charming memoirs, *The Happy Summer Days*, he recalls as a child tasting this "forbidden fruit" in the garden of the villa: "It had a strange bitter taste that seemed to make my teeth shrink; I threw it away in disgust. As always, I was reprimanded and told that, for all I knew, it might have been poisonous."

Sicily used to send barrels of bitter oranges to England to make marmalade, but they are becoming increasingly rare. It is not at all easy for me to find them when I make my marmalade and jam in February. In the past they were cultivated for the purpose of propagating new groves. Now quicker ways have been found.

I make the preserves in the new kitchen at Case Vecchie, which is transformed into a sticky laboratory in no time. Last year I made nearly three thousand jars with my crew, which includes Maria Tartaglia and Sergio Ippolito. Maria is an excellent cook; she often demonstrates her specialties at the cooking school. (She is the one who helped me make the *Estratto di Pomodoro*.) Sergio, a talented young man from Valledolmo, a nearby village, comes to help in our kitchens when he's home on holiday. For the past couple of years, he's been working in other kitchens elsewhere. As a boy, Sergio started by assisting Mario. At first, Mario would send him off on a fool's errand when he was about to do something he didn't want Sergio to see. But then he got to like him, and he trained him.

I learned to make jam and marmalade not from my mother or Mario but from my Swiss nanny, Louise Feuillet. Nanny (pronounced with the accent on the last syllable, as in French) came to us in 1940 when Lucio was born, and we kept in touch with one another even when we were too old to have a nanny and she left. When we were children, we used to spend the month of August with her in her cottage in the woods in the Swiss Alps. My mother would send herbs from Regaleali with us—oregano, rosemary, and bay. The cottage would fill with Sicilian aromas, and Nanny would clap her hands with joy. When our children were old enough, they went there, too, and they had the most marvelous time, picking mushrooms and raspberries in the forest and eating good wholesome food. And learning French, of course.

Nanny loved to take us children into the kitchen. As soon as we were old enough not to cut or burn ourselves or set the house on fire, she taught us how to make such wonderful things as *tarte aux pommes* with a *pâte demi-feuilletée* and apples from the orchard.

Nanny always made marmalade. In later years, when she could not find bitter oranges in her own country, we would send her some, and she would bring jars of marmalade when she came to visit us. When she got very old, I asked her for the recipe. Then, shortly before she died, she sent me some jars of bilberry jam from Switzerland, which I keep as a reminder of her.

I make my marmalades and jams the way Nanny told me. *Marmellata di Pompelmo* is one of the most successful.

MARMELLATA DI POMPELMO *Grapefruit Marmalade*

3 large grapefruits
1 lemon or citron
6 cups water
Sugar

Wash the grapefruits and the lemon or citron and cut all the fruit into quarters. Remove the seeds, if necessary. Slice the fruit crosswise into thin triangles. Put the fruit into a very large nonreactive saucepan with the water. Cover and set aside for 24 hours.

The next day, bring the fruit to a boil and boil vigorously for about 40 to 50 minutes, until the fruit is transparent. Remove from the heat and set aside for another 24 hours.

Weigh the fruit-and-water mixture and measure out the same amount of sugar by weight. Bring the fruit to a boil, stir in the sugar, and bring back to a boil. Cook, stirring from time to time to keep the jam from sticking to the bottom, for about 40 minutes. Reduce the heat if the mixture threatens to boil over. Start testing by placing a spoonful of the mixture on a dish and letting it cool to see if it sets. When it sets, remove it from the heat and stir for about 5 minutes. Pour the marmellata into sterilized jars, leaving about 1/2 inch of space at the top of each jar. Close the jars and turn them upside down to cool. This makes about 5 half-pints of marmellata.

Citrus plays a big role in family life in Sicily, and not just in cooking. I remember how on sunny winter days when I was growing up, the women, dressed in black (they all wore mourning then), would sit in the doorways cleaning copper with lemons. They would sprinkle the pans with sea salt and rub them round and round with half a lemon, scrubbing hard. They would put them out to dry in the sun and later wash and polish them with a cloth. No product you can buy today will make copper shine the way lemon and salt do.

We often cut sprays of citrus flowers to decorate a corner of the house. Around Christmas we pick those with the golden ripe fruit still hanging from them, like balls on a Christmas tree. When I got married back in 1957, brides carried a bouquet of orange blossoms, the symbol of purity. I seldom see that anymore. The lovely fresh orange blossoms have been replaced by bought flowers, more sophisticated perhaps and more costly for sure, but no match when it comes to elegance.

The citrus trees that blossomed in spring start bearing fruit in November, and they keep bearing until May or even June. The wrong time of year, I often think—it is a pity

I like to design centerpieces from whatever nature has to offer. Here, in winter, citrus and olive leaves.

to be deprived of citrus juice in the hot days of summer when you crave it most. There are actually lemons in the shops then, but they are small and dry. So when lemons are in season and plentiful, we squeeze them and freeze the juice to have it in summer.

Citrus is very much part of the flavor of Sicilian cuisine. We are forever using either the juice or the peel. Grated orange or lemon peel goes in practically all our desserts: *Pan di Spagna, Pignoccata, Biscotti Regina,* and brittle. The pastry dough for the classic *Timballo di Pasta Frolla Dolce,* which has a savory filling, is quite sweet and strongly flavored with lemon.

TIMBALLO DI PASTA FROLLA DOLCE *Filled Pastry Timbale*

Pasta Frolla

4 to 4¹/₂ cups flour

1 cup sugar

Grated peel of 2 lemons

Salt

10 ounces butter, cut into ¹/₂-inch pieces

6 egg yolks

Béchamel

2¹/₂ cups milk

1 beef bouillon cube

1 tablespoon butter

1 tablespoon flour

✤

1 pound perciatelli

3 cups Ragoncino (page 134)

4 hard-boiled eggs, peeled and thickly sliced

1 pound fresh mozzarella, thickly sliced

¹/₂ cup chopped prosciutto

¹/₂ cup chopped boiled ham

1 cup grated parmesan

2 egg whites, lightly beaten

Pour the flour out onto a work surface or into a bowl. Make a well in the flour and add the sugar, lemon peel, and 2 pinches of salt. Work the butter into the dough with your fingertips. Add the egg yolks, one by one, working them into the dough. Avoid overworking the dough. Once it is smooth and even, wrap it in plastic and put it in the refrigerator to rest.

For the béchamel, heat the milk and dissolve the bouillon cube in it. Set aside. Melt the tablespoon of butter in a small saucepan and remove from the heat. Stir in the flour and put the pan back on the heat. Add the milk gradually, whisking to prevent lumps from forming. Continue to cook, whisking constantly, until the béchamel thickens.

Preheat the oven to 375°F. Butter a 10-inch springform pan and dust it with flour.

Cook the perciatelli in boiling salted water until al dente. Drain thoroughly and mix with the béchamel and the ragoncino.

Roll out half of the pastry and put it into the pan, allowing the pastry to hang over the rim. Press against the bottom and sides of the pan. Spread the bottom with half of the pasta mixture. Cover that with the eggs and the mozzarella. Combine the prosciutto and boiled ham with half the parmesan and spread this evenly over the eggs and mozzarella. Finish with the remaining pasta mixture and sprinkle the remaining parmesan on top.

Roll out about three-fourths of the remaining dough into a circle slightly larger than the pan. Cover the pasta with the dough, trim any excess dough from the top and the sides, and fold the overhanging dough up and over. Crimp to seal. Decorate the top with the sign of the sun or the moon cut from the remaining pastry and place it in the center. Brush with the beaten egg whites. Place the timballo in the oven, reduce the temperature to 350°F., and bake for 45 minutes, until the pastry is golden. This rich timballo serves 10 to 12 as a first course.

I'll never forget the time Giovanni Carpinello, a great amateur cook whose specialty is the *timballo*, made it for a group of my American friends who did not want to leave Sicily without tasting it—and especially not without a recipe. We all crowded into his kitchen at Borragine, not far from Regaleali, for the demonstration. He launched into it with his customary enthusiasm, and we had to make him pause over and over again to take a measurement or write down an important detail.

When he finished, there was a little bit of everything left over, so he boiled up some dog macaroni—they make special pasta for pets in Italy; it even comes in different shapes, just like pasta for people—and wiped the pot we had used for the béchamel clean with it. Then he threw in a few pieces of stale bread, some *ragoncino*, and the extra egg whites from the *pasta frolla*, mixed it all up, and put it outside his kitchen door for the dogs. The cats, about a dozen of them, got to it first, but there was enough for the whole menagerie.

We also use lemon peel to make one of the classic tisanes, the *Canarino* (Lemon Tisane), so-called because of its canary-yellow color. To make it, you put about two cups of water in a *pentolino* (small pot) with the peel of half a lemon and bring it to a boil for two minutes. You can add a fresh bay leaf, too. The tisane has to stand for another two minutes before being poured.

Costanza is the tisane expert of the family; she brews some extraordinary ones, with bay leaves, mint, lemon balm, and other herbs. She is also a very good cook; hers is the best risotto in the whole family. When I have a group at the cooking school, she gives a dinner, always with risotto as the first course. She makes her risotto with a good home-made broth and adds mushrooms or artichokes—or marrow, as they do in Milan.

The second course is cheese and salad, a tasting of all our cheeses, from fresh ricotta to *tuma* (curd cheese) to *primo sale* (young pecorino) to pecorino, usually with *Insalata Verde Mista con gli Agrumi*. When I don't have salad greens, I make *Insalata di Spinaci alla Siciliana* (Spinach Salad with Pine Nuts and Currants). I dress some freshly picked tender leaves of spinach with a sauce made of grapefruit pieces lightly pressed with a fork to extract the juice, wine vinegar, olive oil, salt, and ground hot pepper and toss the salad with pine nuts and currants.

Costanza and I are very close. We were born only eleven months apart, and we grew up like twins. We were even dressed alike, she in pale blue, to match the color of her eyes, and I in pink. Until we got married, we did everything together, and we still share the same ideas on the important things in life. She is the sweetest person you could ever hope to meet, always kind and agreeable. Zia Maria, my mother's sister, calls her Switzerland, because she never takes sides.

Lemon is used in a quick spaghetti dish called *Pasta al Limone* (Spaghetti with Lemon). You prepare a sauce of sautéed garlic and parsley with lemon juice while waiting for the water to boil for the spaghetti. Sometimes cream is added, but I think the nice thing about this dish is the freshness and purity of the ingredients.

Lemon juice is often squeezed on meat that is to be roasted or grilled. We also roast chicken with citrus. For *Pollo al Forno al Limone* (Roast Chicken with Lemon), we stick a couple of lemons (pierced with a fork) and bouillon cubes into the cavity of a chicken and roast it in a hot oven, basting it from time to time with the pan juices, until it's done. For *Pollo al Forno all'Arancia* (Roast Chicken with Orange), we put the chicken into the pan with one thickly sliced onion, the juice of two or three oranges, half a cup of wine, and rosemary, salt, and pepper to taste and roast it in a hot oven, basting often.

Citrus is wonderful in salad. *Insalata di Finocchio e Cedro* (Fennel and Citron Salad) is a typical winter salad. Citron is most often candied, but in this dish it is combined raw with fennel, one of the few vegetables Sicilians will eat raw. I love fennel, and I often have it plain, just sprinkled with salt, at the end of the meal, like a piece of fruit. It is an old Sicilian custom.

For the salad you take two fennel bulbs, cut them in half lengthwise, and slice them

Panierini di Mandarino (page 222).

very thin. Peel a citron, leaving on the thick white pith. (The flesh and pith of the citron are in perfect harmony when eaten together.) Quarter the citron and slice it very thin. Combine with the fennel and dress the salad with a vinaigrette. Fresh thyme sprinkled on top makes it very special.

Another excellent citrus salad is *Insalata di Arance e Olive Nere* (Black Olive and Orange Salad). It's very attractive and tasty, yet it's nothing more than sliced peeled oranges, sliced onions, and pitted black olives in a vinaigrette.

The most famous citrus dessert at Regaleali is *Panierini di Mandarino*, which Mario often makes when we expect guests. He cuts out handles on a few of the tangerines, removes the "lids" of the rest, and scoops out the pulp. Then he sets these tangerine baskets aside in a plastic bag in the refrigerator. He makes gelatin and fills the shells with it and puts the lids back on when it's time to serve.

PANIERINI DI MANDARINO *Tangerine Baskets*

6 tangerines, with stems and leaves attached
3 envelopes unflavored gelatin
1 1/2 cups cold water
1 cup freshly squeezed orange juice
1 cup freshly squeezed tangerine juice
1/4 cup freshly squeezed lemon juice
1 cup sugar

Make the tangerine baskets by cutting 2 wedge-shaped pieces out of the upper third of each tangerine, leaving a 1/3-inch strip over the top to form a handle. Carefully extract the pulp and save for juicing. Set the baskets aside until ready to use. You can prepare them a day or two ahead and store them in a plastic bag in the refrigerator.

Soften the gelatin by soaking it in 1/2 cup of the water in a medium saucepan. Add the fruit juices, the sugar, and the remaining cup of water. Bring the mixture to a boil over high heat, whisking it to dissolve the gelatin. Boil for about 1 minute and remove the gelatin from the heat.

Filter the gelatin mixture through a wet paper towel or a clean kitchen towel into a bowl. (For very clear gelatin, use a thick kitchen towel.) Cover the bowl with plastic wrap and put it into the refrigerator for at least 4 hours or overnight to jell.

Just before serving, remove the gelatin from the refrigerator, stir it to break it up, and spoon it into the baskets. This makes 6 tangerine baskets.

Rice

The Arabs brought rice to Sicily. It was cultivated in parts of eastern Sicily until the eighteenth century. Something must have happened then, most likely a change in climate leading to a lack of water, because now the only rice we see is in boxes on the shelves of shops. It is from northern Italy, where there are vast rice plantations. I have specified Arborio rice in my recipes because that's what we use at Regaleali for rice dishes that start with a risotto base: *Arancine*, *Ghineffi di Riso*, and *Cappuccetti di Riso*.

All risotto is made the same way. The grains of rice are coated with fat and then liquid is stirred into the pot little by little, until the rice is smooth and creamy but the individual grains are al dente. The fat and the liquid can vary, though we usually use butter, sometimes butter and margarine, and broth. If the risotto is to be served as a first course, we make it with homemade broth.

One winter, Luigi Perrotta from the family-owned Hotel Adelaide in Naples came to Regaleali with two of his cooks for courses at the cooking school. They were so enchanted by the abundance of citrus that they invented *Risotto agli Agrumi* on the spot.

RISOTTO AGLI AGRUMI *Risotto with Citrus Fruit*

1/2 grapefruit

1 orange

1 onion, finely chopped

4 tablespoons butter

1 pound Arborio rice

3/4 cup white wine

6 cups homemade beef broth

1/2 cup grated parmesan

Peel the grapefruit and orange, reserving the peel and leaving the white pith on the fruit. Julienne enough peel to make 2 tablespoons of strips. Boil the strips in a cup or so of water for 3 minutes. Drain and set aside.

Remove the pith from the fruit, working over a bowl to catch the juices. Separate enough of the pulp from the membranes to make 3/4 cup of pulp. Set aside, reserving the best pieces for garnishing.

Sauté the onion in 2 tablespoons of the butter for 2 to 3 minutes, until transparent. Add the rice and stir well to coat the grains. Add the wine, and continue cooking until the wine evaporates, about 2 minutes. Add half of the julienned peel, and begin adding the broth, ladleful by ladleful, waiting until each is absorbed before adding the next. Cook, stirring constantly. After about 10 minutes, add half of the fruit pulp, half of the juices that have accumulated in the bowl, and the remaining julienned peel. Continue cooking for about 10 more minutes, until the rice is done but still al dente. Remove the rice from the heat, and stir in the parmesan, the remaining butter, and the remaining pulp and juices. Garnish with the reserved fruit and serve. This serves 6 to 8 as a first course.

If the risotto is part of another dish, we make the broth with bouillon cubes. For *Ghineffi di Riso*, we also add saffron for its characteristic color and flavor. Everyone likes these little golden rice cubes, to eat first as a snack, then in consommé.

CONSOMME *Consommé*

2 pounds beef shanks or shin meat, trimmed and cut into 2-inch pieces
1 onion, peeled
1 carrot
1 stalk celery
2 beef bouillon cubes
3 egg whites, beaten
Salt
Ghineffi di Riso (recipe follows)
Grated parmesan, for garnish (optional)

Put the meat in a medium stockpot and add the onion, carrot, celery, and bouillon cubes. Add water to cover by at least 1 inch. Bring the pot to a boil, reduce the heat to very low, and cook for about 2 hours. Strain the consommé through a colander lined with a moist cheesecloth and discard the vegetables.

Pour the consommé back into a medium saucepan, whisk in the beaten egg whites, and bring to a boil. When the egg whites come to the surface and foam, turn off the heat. Remove the egg whites quickly and carefully. Season to taste with salt. Serve warm, garnished with Ghineffi di Riso and parmesan, if you like, or cool. This makes 6 cups.

GHINEFFI DI RISO *Fried Rice Cubes*

2 tablespoons margarine

4 tablespoons butter

1 pound Arborio rice

2 beef bouillon cubes, dissolved in 8 cups boiling water

8 saffron threads or ¹/₂ teaspoon powdered saffron

¹/₄ cup grated parmesan

2 egg yolks, beaten

Salt

¹/₂ cup flour

1 egg, beaten with 2 teaspoons water, for egg wash

¹/₂ cup breadcrumbs

Oil, for frying

Melt the margarine and 2 tablespoons of the butter in a large saucepan and add the rice, stirring until well coated. Stir in the bouillon ladleful by ladleful, waiting until each is absorbed before adding the next. When the risotto has cooked about 10 minutes, add the saffron. Continue adding bouillon and cooking until the risotto is smooth and creamy, with an al dente consistency. There may be some bouillon left over.

Add the remaining butter and the parmesan and stir to blend. Transfer the risotto to a large bowl and set it in a cold-water bath. Add the beaten egg yolks as soon as the risotto is no longer hot enough to cook them. Taste and add salt if needed.

Spread the risotto out on a buttered surface and flatten to about ³/₄ inch. Let it cool. Cut the rice into ³/₄-inch squares. Pour the flour, egg wash, and breadcrumbs into separate soup bowls. Dip the cubes first in the flour, then in the egg wash, and then in the breadcrumbs. Set aside until all are done.

Heat 1¹/₂ inches of oil in a deep sauté pan. Test by dipping in one of the rice cubes. It should sizzle. Fry the cubes until golden and drain on paper towels. This makes enough for 6 to 8 people to eat some as a snack and put the rest in consommé.

The filling for *Cappuccetti di Riso* is also tinged with saffron. The *Agglassato* sauce is a simplified *glace*, the reduced sauce of a piece of beef braised in red wine with aromatic vegetables. The method is the same as for the veal for the *Vitello Tonné*, but the sauce is stronger, since it is made with red wine rather than white and with beef bouillon cubes. We have the meat hot with sauce in winter, cold as part of *Carne Fredda Mista* in summer.

We use the sauce a lot, on spaghetti or rice or with potatoes—also on top of poached eggs. Even the children, when they are naughty and refuse to eat, will eat anything if Mario puts *Agglassato* sauce on it.

CAPPUCCETTI DI RISO *Risotto-Stuffed Cabbage Rolls*

1 large head cabbage
1/2 cup minced onion
4 tablespoons butter
1 cup Arborio rice
2 beef bouillon cubes, dissolved in 3 1/2 cups boiling water
8 saffron threads or 1/2 teaspoon powdered saffron
1 cup chopped boiled ham
3/4 cup grated parmesan
Grated nutmeg
Salt
Black pepper
1 cup Agglassato sauce (recipe follows)

Trim the cabbage and cut it into quarters. Boil it in salted water until tender but still firm. Drain the cabbage and soak it in cold water until cool.

Sauté the onion in 2 tablespoons of the butter. Add the rice and sauté, stirring until all the grains are coated. Begin adding the bouillon ladleful by ladleful, waiting until each is absorbed before adding the next. When the risotto is half-cooked, add the saffron dissolved in a ladleful of bouillon. Continue adding bouillon and stirring until the risotto is smooth and creamy with an al dente consistency. Mix in 1 tablespoon of the remaining butter, 1/2 cup of the ham, 1/2 cup of the parmesan, and a pinch of nutmeg. Add salt and pepper to taste. Spread out the risotto to cool.

Preheat the oven to 350°F. Grease an 8×10-inch baking dish with butter.

Separate the cabbage leaves and remove the tough ribs. Overlap 2 leaves to form a base. Fill with 1 heaping teaspoon of risotto and wrap to form a round bundle about 1 1/2 inches wide. Place the bundles, seam side down, close together in the baking dish. Sprinkle with the remaining chopped ham and parmesan and dot with the remaining butter. Bake for 20 to 30 minutes, or until lightly browned. Serve with Agglassato sauce on the side. This serves 6 to 8 as a first course.

AGGLASSATO *Braised Beef*

3 pounds beef, rump or bottom round roast, tied

¼ cup olive oil

3 medium onions, chopped

2 cups red wine

1 stalk celery

1 small carrot

2 or 3 sprigs parsley

1 sprig rosemary

2 beef bouillon cubes

1 tablespoon flour, mixed with ¼ cup water

Salt

Black pepper

Brown the meat in the olive oil on all sides in a heavy casserole. Add the onions and sauté until they are soft. Add some of the wine, scraping to deglaze the casserole. Add water almost to cover. Tie together the celery, carrot, parsley, and rosemary and add to the casserole with the bouillon cubes and the rest of the wine. Stir in the flour-water slurry. Bring to a boil, reduce the heat, and simmer, covered, for 1 to 1½ hours, until the meat is tender.

Remove the meat and let it cool thoroughly. Remove and discard the bundle of vegetables and herbs. Pass the sauce through a food mill. Reduce it in a saucepan over medium heat until it has thickened to the consistency of cream. Add salt and pepper to taste.

Slice the meat when it's cold. Serve cold. Or, to serve it warm, reconstruct the roast by running 1 or 2 skewers through it to hold the slices in place. Reheat it in the sauce. This serves 4 to 6 as a main course.

The children also love *Riso Legato*, a simple soup with an egg liaison. Then again, we all love it; it reminds us of our childhood. When you make this soup, take care that the broth is not boiling hot and be sure to pour it slowly into the liaison, so that the soup doesn't curdle.

Cured black and green table olives make good salads. Olives are raked from the trees by men on ladders. The olives used to be stuffed into hemp baskets for pressing; now they go directly to the mill in town and the oil is returned to us for bottling. At Christmastime I fill baskets with bottles of oil, Regaleali wine, and jars of my preserved food.

RISO LEGATO *Rice Soup*

6 cups Consomme (page 224)
1 cup cooked rice
1 egg yolk
¼ cup milk
2 tablespoons butter
¼ cup grated parmesan
Salt
Black pepper

Heat the Consomme and add the rice to warm it. Whisk together the egg yolk, milk, butter, and parmesan in the bottom of a soup tureen. Whisk in the broth, slowly at first, then pour it in. Add salt and pepper to taste. Serve immediately. This serves 4 as a first course.

‖ *Olives* ‖

The birthplace of the olive tree is shrouded in myth and legend, but wherever it originated, it has spread all over the Mediterranean basin, including Sicily. Since time immemorial, its fruit has provided man with nourishment and even light in the days when oil was burned in lamps. The tree itself is surely one of nature's masterpieces. It grows very slowly and lives for centuries. People who know the olive say each tree has its own personality. The groves of olive trees at Regaleali, with their thick, twisted trunks and luxuriant foliage, which turns silver when the wind ruffles the green and gray leaves, are an unforgettable sight.

When the trees bloom in June, they are covered with very tiny white blossoms that look like tufts of cotton wool. Warm days are good for the olive at that moment, since the heat helps in setting fruit. Not all the little olives will ripen; it depends on the weather during the growing season. Usually a tree bears every other year, but it is rare not to pick a single olive, as happened in 1990, the third year of a devastating drought.

There are essentially two kinds of olives, those grown for oil and those grown for the table. Green and black olives are, of course, not different varieties; all olives are green when unripe and black when mature. We pick green table olives in September and October. To preserve them, we make a *salamoia* (brine solution), which is tested with an egg; when the balance of salt and water is correct, the egg floats. We add garlic, hot peppers, and bay leaves to the brine, put in the olives, and cover them completely with braided stalks of wild fennel. The olives are left like this for four months until mid-winter. We take out as much as we want at a time, rinse them thoroughly, and prepare them as *Olive Verdi Condite.*

OLIVE VERDI CONDITE *Seasoned Green Olives*

³/₄ pound cured green olives

¹/₂ small red onion, sliced

1 stalk celery with some tender leaves, chopped

1 garlic clove, minced

2 tablespoons dried oregano

1 small hot pepper, chopped

2 tablespoons white wine vinegar

³/₄ cup olive oil

Rinse the olives to remove excess salt, and shake them dry. Put the olives in a medium bowl with the onion, celery, garlic, oregano, and hot pepper. Mix with the vinegar and olive oil. Serve at room temperature. This makes 2 cups of seasoned olives.

Another style of seasoning for green olives is called *Olive del Monaco* (Olives Monk's Style). For this we use vinegar, sugar, and fresh herbs, especially mint but also sage and rosemary.

If we don't want to wait so long to eat the olives, we prepare *Olive Schiacciate in Salamoia* (Smashed Olives in Brine). We smash the olives and put them in fresh clean water for forty-eight hours, changing the water every twelve hours. Then we steep the olives in a simple *salamoia* for at least four days. My father likes them at that point, but they are very bitter; for my personal taste, I would leave them for a week. We remove the olives from the brine, pit them, and season them as for *Olive Verdi Condite.* These olives have to be eaten within a month; after that they go soft. When we use this method of preparation, we do several batches at different intervals so that we always have some on hand for unexpected guests.

Black table olives are picked just when they turn black, usually around the end of November. Being ripe and delicate, they have to be handled with great care. We choose the best and put them in large flat baskets with salt to draw off the juices. On the first day, we turn them continuously, after that only now and then. It takes twenty to twenty-five days for them to be sufficiently dried. Some people have an eye for it and can tell the exact moment when the olives are ready. They are rinsed in clean water and spread out on screens to dry in the sun for a couple of days. Then we put them in jars and cover them with oil. They keep forever. We use these olives for *Broccoli con Olive Nere, Insalata di Arance e Olive Nere,* and bread with olives. We also prepare some as *Olive Nere Condite.*

OLIVE NERE CONDITE *Seasoned Black Olives*

³/₄ pound oil-cured black olives
1 teaspoon rosemary needles
Grated peel of 1 orange (optional)
2 garlic cloves, crushed
1 small hot pepper, chopped
¹/₂ cup olive oil

Put the olives in a bowl and add the rosemary, orange peel, if using, garlic, and hot pepper. Mix with the olive oil. Serve at room temperature. This makes 2 cups of seasoned olives.

The best olives you can ever eat are the ones we call *passoloni.* These are the olives every Sicilian dreams of. They are a particular variety of olive of the kind used for oil; they are left on the tree to mature and are picked in December. By then they're black and wrinkled, like tiny prunes; they can be eaten straight from the tree. They have a slightly bitter taste, but incredible! *Passoloni* are not cured or seasoned, and they keep for only a very short time.

Those are the ways we have of preserving olives at Regaleali as I remember them all my life. Other people have other ways, and some may even be better; olives are a very popular dish. Wherever you go in the country, if a Sicilian, rich or poor, offers you something to eat, there will always be olives—olives with cheese and bread and wine.

Olive Oil

The olives for oil are picked just before they start turning dark. That happens sometimes as early as the week of San Martino, sometimes not until much, much later.

In years past, Sicilian peasants used to make a coarse oil from fully ripe black olives. They believed that since it had a strong flavor, they could use less, and therefore it would last longer. But this was also the only kind of oil they knew how to make. At the time, people thought that very ripe olives would give more oil because if you squeeze one just before it starts to wrinkle, a drop of oil will spread on your fingers. But the ripe olives were very easily damaged. Besides, they were kept too long before crushing, and so fermentation set in. The resulting oil did not have the transparency and finesse we now expect. Today's markets and palates are more sophisticated and demand the very best.

For good oil, the olives must be picked by hand. Olive picking is one of the most labor-intensive—and expensive—operations in agriculture. It is also very hard work.

In the traditional method, which we use, nets are placed under the trees and the men go up on ladders and comb the olives off the branches with their hands and a short-handled rake. In another method, the branches are beaten with long flexible sticks; this is faster but good farmers usually don't like to do it because it risks damaging the trees. Either way, the olives shower down to the nets, along with twigs and leaves and other debris, which has to be removed before the olives are pressed. The cleaned olives are gathered in baskets and transported to the nearest mill by tractor or truck. At this point, it is critical to get the olives to the mill quickly, before fermentation sets in.

In the old days, we had our own oil mill at Regaleali. Everything was done by hand. With the advent of electricity, which came late because we are so far inland, things went faster, but it was still the same process as before. The olives were brought to the basement of the mill, where they were crushed with a grindstone. Then the paste was stuffed into loosely woven hemp *fiscoli* (baskets). These were stacked, alternating with tightly woven hemp press pads to equalize the pressure, on a screw press. Long ago, the press was turned by four men, then by mules, and later by electricity.

The *fiore dell'olio* (olive must), mixed with water, ran down from under the press into a trough. The dirt and water, being heavier, sank to the bottom. A man who was expert at the task stood by with a long-handled ladle and scooped off the oil that came to the surface and poured it into a *giara* (glazed oil jar). When only a little oil was left floating on the water, the ladle was replaced with a skimmer, and the man ran after every last drop of oil. It sounds easy, but it took a lot of skill. The oil was left to stand for about two weeks, to decant. This last operation was repeated three or four times until the oil was clear and all the *feccia* (dregs) had settled to the bottom. (The dregs were used for a homemade soft soap that was the best remedy for bad stains; it is now made commercially.)

When the wine cellars were renovated in 1965, the old oil mill had to give way to the winery. Now we send our olives to an electrified stone mill in Vallelunga, and the next day delicious green oil comes back in stainless-steel containers. We started bottling it for sale in 1993.

It is always exciting to taste the new oil. The best way is to dip a piece of fresh home-made bread right in it. All the natural flavors shine, and you can really test the purity of the oil and appreciate all the hard work that went into making it.

Christmas

Preparations for Christmas begin far in advance. Weeks ahead we send off our Christmas presents, mostly bottles of wine. For special friends I make baskets with some of my preserved foods, which have their own distinctive label. It says "Case Vecchie" and "Anna Tasca Lanza" and shows my little house with its rampant rose. In the middle of each basket I place a small pecorino cheese tied with a big red bow. Then I tuck in jars of *Pomodori Seccati al Sole* and preserved mushrooms, eggplant, and tuna, some *Cotognata*, honey, and, of course, wine. I always make the marmalade that I include in my Christmas baskets from the recipe Nanny gave me.

Soon the family, scattered now, begins to gather. Each family stays in a separate house, but all of us Tasca children and grandchildren—and great-grandchildren now—get together in the Case Grandi at mealtimes, and Mario cooks for everyone. My mother remembers all our favorite dishes, and it's always the same—you get up from the table thinking you won't ever be able to touch food again.

On Christmas Eve, we celebrate Mass in the chapel at five in the afternoon. Costanza plays the organ, and we all sing Christmas carols. Then we walk back to the salon at the Case Grandi for the Christmas party. In the corner, a tall tree decorated with gold and silver ribbons reaches to the ceiling. Underneath it are mountains of presents, which we open before dinner so that the children can join in the festivities before going to bed. Opposite the tree at the far end of the room a crackling fire burns in the fireplace.

The salon was the granary in my grandfather's day and later the bottling room when we started bottling the wine. When we were renovating the room, my father wanted to install a ceramic coat of arms over the mantel. We all thought it would be too heavy, but he was very insistent. Luckily, our good friends Beatrice and Giovanni Carpinello came to visit at just the right moment. I asked Bice to make a drawing that would fill the space and have it ready in time for my parents' fiftieth anniversary party, which was to take place soon afterward. She did a lovely painting, and my father could not refuse such a beautiful present.

On Christmas Day, we have lunch in the salon. We set the central table, creating a long buffet. My father and mother sit opposite each other halfway down, with their children, grandchildren, and great-grandchildren—some sitting on cushions, others in high chairs—on either side. Sometimes it seems as if there is no difference in age between my parents and the little ones as they join in all their childish jokes and games, just as they did with us many years ago.

We start the meal with *Spuma di Fegatini,* and for the first course have a choice of *Sformato di Formaggio Principe di Galles* and *Pasta alla Moda dei Monzù*. Both are very rich, but some people can't resist having a taste of each.

PASTA ALLA MODA DEI MONZÙ *Pasta with Truffles and Cream*

One 6- to 8-ounce chicken breast
$^1/_2$ cup julienned boiled ham
1 small black truffle, sliced
$^1/_3$ cup grated parmesan
Béchamel
    1 beef bouillon cube
    $2^1/_2$ cups milk
    4 tablespoons butter
    1 tablespoon flour
    Salt
    Black pepper
    ✧
1 pound rigatoni or egg pappardelle
$^1/_4$ cup heavy cream, whipped
Grated parmesan, for garnish

Cook the chicken breast in boiling salted water for 10 minutes. Drain, remove and discard the skin and bones, and cut the meat in julienne strips. Put the pieces of chicken in a small bowl, add the ham, truffle, and the parmesan, and set aside.

For the béchamel, put the bouillon cube in the milk and heat to dissolve. Do not boil. Melt the butter in a medium saucepan, remove it from the heat, and whisk in the flour. Gradually whisk in the milk, return it to the heat, and cook, stirring constantly, until the béchamel is thickened, about 20 minutes. Season to taste with salt and pepper.

Cook the pasta in boiling salted water until tender. Drain and mix with the béchamel and half the chicken mixture. Put the remaining chicken mixture on top and decorate with the whipped cream. Serve immediately. Pass grated parmesan at the table. This rich pasta serves 4 as a first course.

For the main course, we always have *Tacchino al Forno con Panata* and *Sella di Agnello al Cognac*. To accompany them is a *Sformato di Spinaci*.

OVERLEAF: *The vineyards in winter look barren, but still the hillsides are green.*

Tacchino al Forno con Panata
Roast Turkey with Sicilian Bread Stuffing

2 cups chopped onion

1 cup olive oil

3/4 pound sandwich bread, crusts removed, cut into 1/4-inch dice (5 cups)

3/4 pound boiled ham, cut into 1/4-inch dice

1/2 pound Gouda, cut into 1/4-inch dice

1/2 pound Emmenthaler, cut into 1/4-inch dice

1/2 cup minced parsley

8 egg yolks

Salt

Black pepper

One 16-pound turkey, dressed

1/4 cup rosemary needles

Sauté the onion in the olive oil until just golden, about 4 to 5 minutes. Put the bread, ham, cheeses, and parsley into a large bowl and pour the olive oil–onion mixture on top. Add the egg yolks and season with salt and pepper to taste. Stir and set aside. The mixture should be quite moist.

Preheat the oven to 300°F.

Season the cavities of the turkey with salt and pepper. Stuff the neck, then the abdominal cavity. Sew up the turkey, oil it with additional olive oil, and season it with salt and pepper to taste and the rosemary. Roast the turkey for about 12 minutes per pound, until the juices run clear, basting every 30 minutes. When the turkey is done, turn off the oven, leaving the door ajar to allow the turkey to rest for at least 30 minutes. Carve and serve. This serves 10 to 12 as a main course.

SELLA DI AGNELLO AL COGNAC
Saddle of Lamb with a Cognac Cream Sauce

One 4½-pound saddle of lamb, well trimmed

⅓ cup olive oil

Salt

Black pepper

1 tablespoon rosemary needles

2 medium onions, quartered

3 garlic cloves, peeled

8 tablespoons butter

1 cup heavy cream

½ cup cognac or brandy

3 tablespoons flour, mixed with ¾ cup water

Preheat the oven to 400°F.

Put the lamb, loin side up, in a roasting pan. Rub with half of the olive oil and season with salt, pepper, and rosemary. Put the onions and garlic in the pan. Roast the lamb for 30 to 35 minutes, slide it out of the oven, and douse it with the remaining olive oil. Return it to the oven and roast for about 20 minutes more, until well done, not at all pink. Remove the lamb to a cutting board and keep it warm.

Pour off all but about 2 tablespoons of the fat in the pan and deglaze the pan with water. Puree the contents of the roasting pan, including the garlic and onions, in a food mill or food processor until quite smooth. Transfer the puree to a saucepan, add the butter, cream, and cognac, and bring to a boil. Reduce the heat. Whisk the flour-water slurry into the sauce. Simmer, stirring frequently, until the sauce is thickened, about 15 minutes. Taste the sauce for seasoning and set it aside.

Cut the meat away from the bone and cut each piece in half crosswise. Slice the meat lengthwise ½ inch thick. Place the loin strips back on the bones, reassembling the saddle. Add the tenderloin pieces from the underside here and there. Cover the meat with some of the sauce and pass the rest in a sauceboat. Serve the lamb warm. This serves 6 to 8 as a main course.

Miniature Cannoli disappear in two bites.

Patate Schiacciate al Forno are good with *Tacchino al Forno con Panata* or *Sella di Agnello al Cognac* or just about any kind of roast. Once when Mario made these potato patties in Washington, D.C., there were only Red Bliss potatoes. Mario was very suspicious because they weren't yellow like ours; in fact, I think he suspected they weren't potatoes at all. But they worked very well.

PATATE SCHIACCIATE AL FORNO *Mario's Potatoes*

Twelve 2- to 3-inch potatoes
Salt
Black pepper

Wash the potatoes. Cook in boiling salted water until almost done, 15 to 20 minutes. (Do not cook the potatoes until they are done or they will break apart when you pound them.) Drain, cool, and peel.

Place a potato in the corner of a clean dish towel, twist and hold the towel in one hand, and, using a meat pounder or the back of a frying pan, flatten the potato into a cake about $1/2$ inch thick. Season the potato cakes with salt and pepper.

About 30 minutes before serving, preheat the oven to 350°F. Lightly grease a baking sheet with olive oil.

Place the potatoes on the baking sheet and bake until golden, turning once, about 20 minutes. Serve warm. This serves 6 as a side dish.

The dessert buffet is crowded with all the cakes and pastries that were given to us as Christmas presents. Mario makes *Pignoccata*, *Cannoli* so small they disappear in a mouthful, and *Buccellato*, short-dough pastry filled with dried and candied fruits and pine nuts. Some *buccellati* have more filling, others less. It used to depend on how prosperous the family was. Poor families, for instance, would fill theirs with figs, which are available to everyone in Sicily for the picking; rich families used raisins. The shape also varies—some *buccellati* are round or oval; others are wreath shaped with a white glaze and candy confetti on top. *Buccellato* is the universal taste of Christmas in Sicily.

CANNOLI *Cannoli*

1²/₃ cups flour
2 tablespoons butter
1 teaspoon vinegar
¹/₂ to ³/₄ cup water
1 egg white, lightly beaten
Oil, for frying
1¹/₂ cups Crema di Ricotta (page 63)
Candied fruit, for garnish

Mix together the flour and butter until crumbly. Add the vinegar and mix. Add just enough water to make the dough stick together. It should be somewhat stiff.

Flour the dough and roll it out about $1/4$ inch thick. Cut the dough in half and pass each half through the widest setting on a pasta machine several times, folding it over on itself each time, until smooth. Wrap the pieces in plastic and set aside to rest for at least 1 hour.

Divide the pieces in half. (While working with one portion, keep the rest covered with plastic wrap.) Flour 1 portion of dough and pass it through the pasta machine, beginning with the widest setting and going to the next-to-smallest setting. Lay the strip of dough on a floured surface and cover with plastic wrap. Repeat with the remaining dough. Measure a cannoli tube and use a cannoli cutter or small bowl to cut a circle 1 to 1^1/$_2$ inches smaller than the length of the tube. Roll the dough circle into an oval.

Wrap the dough oval around a cannoli tube. Seal with egg white. Avoid spilling egg on the tube because it will make the pastry stick to the tube. Continue until all the molds are wrapped with dough. Cover any remaining dough with plastic wrap.

Heat 3 inches of oil in a deep fryer or a large pan to about 350° F

Fry the Cannoli in batches until golden. Drain them on paper towels. Remove the Cannoli from the tubes while they are still warm by grasping the end of the cannoli tube with a pot holder and pulling the pastry off the tube. Use several thicknesses of paper towels to protect your fingers and work quickly while the Cannoli are still hot. Cool the Cannoli on paper towels and store them, if not using them right away, in an airtight container. Allow the tubes to cool completely, then continue until all the dough is used.

Fill the Cannoli shells with the crema no more than 1 hour before serving. Garnish with candied fruit. This makes about 16 large Cannoli.

BUCCELLATO *Christmas Wreath*

4 cups flour
Pinch of salt
^{1}/$_4$ teaspoon baking powder
1 cup sugar
^{1}/$_2$ pound butter, cut into ^{1}/$_2$-inch dice
^{1}/$_4$ cup milk
4 large egg yolks, at room temperature
2 large eggs, at room temperature
1 teaspoon vanilla extract

Ripieno di Frutta Secca

^{3}/$_4$ pound dried figs, raisins, or other dried fruit
^{1}/$_4$ cup pine nuts
^{1}/$_2$ cup candied fruit
3 tablespoons thick apricot or plum jam
↚
1 egg beaten with 2 teaspoons water, for egg wash

Combine the flour, salt, baking powder, and sugar on a work surface or in a bowl. Work the butter into the flour until the mixture is crumbly. Make a well in the center and add the milk, egg yolks, eggs, and vanilla and work the dough until it's smooth.

Wrap in plastic and refrigerate for at least 30 minutes to rest.

Meanwhile, make the ripieno. Combine and chop the dried fruit, pine nuts, and candied fruit by hand or in a food processor, pulsing until they are roughly chopped. Stir in the jam by hand. The filling should be thick and quite stiff. Set it aside.

Preheat the oven to 350°F. Line a baking sheet with parchment paper or foil.

Remove the dough from the refrigerator and roll it out into an 18×24-inch rectangle, using a bit of flour to prevent it from sticking. Shape the filling into a log 23 inches long and put it in the center of the dough, leaving a 1/2-inch border at each end. Roll the dough over the filling and pinch it to seal. Carefully transfer the roll to the baking sheet and shape it into a circle, pinching and smoothing the ends of the dough together to join them. Make diagonal slashes along the top of the roll, cutting all the way through to the filling.

Bake the Buccellato for 30 minutes, remove it from the oven, and brush it with the egg wash. Return the ring to the oven and continue baking for about 30 minutes, until the pastry is nicely browned. Serve at room temperature. This serves 20 to 25 people.

While the children are at Regaleali, Mario is sure to make *Profiteroles* with *Crema di Cioccolata* for them. They love the chocolate-coated cream puffs. No matter how many he makes, they beg for more.

PROFITEROLES *Profiteroles*

1 recipe Pâte à Choux (page 62)
1/2 cup heavy cream, whipped
1 cup Crema di Cioccolata (recipe follows)

Preheat the oven to 425°F. Line a 12×18-inch baking sheet with parchment paper.

Fill a pastry bag with the Pâte à Choux. Squeeze the dough onto the baking sheet in 1-inch-high mounds about 1 1/2 inches apart.

Bake for about 20 minutes, until the puffs have doubled in size and are a nice golden color. Turn off the oven and remove the puffs. Slash the side of each puff to release the steam. Return to the oven for about 5 minutes to dry. Remove from the oven and cool on a rack. Fill with the whipped cream and coat with hot crema. Pass the remaining crema in a bowl. This serves 8.

CREMA DI CIOCCOLATA *Chocolate Sauce*

4¼ cups milk
½ cup cornstarch
2 to 2½ cups sugar
1 teaspoon vanilla extract
2 cups Dutch-process cocoa

Pour 4 cups of the milk into a medium saucepan and whisk in the cornstarch, sugar, vanilla, and cocoa. Put the pan over medium heat and continue whisking to avoid lumps. Bring the sauce to a boil, stirring constantly. Allow the sauce to boil for 1 minute, remove it from the heat, and stir it for 2 minutes longer. If the sauce is too thick, use some of the remaining milk to thin it. This makes 4 cups of crema. This sauce keeps well in a covered jar in the refrigerator.

Winter in Sicily is short, but it seems long,

perhaps because of the absence of the sun's warmth, which

we are so accustomed to. When the sun shines after a

few rainy or cloudy days, the colors seem incredibly vivid.

I always run out to the garden to see if there is

something new, but usually nothing has changed.

In nature, we have to wait for every living

thing's time to come. The first harbinger of spring is a short

blue iris, bright, bright blue, with many leaves.

Then come the almond blossoms in February, and the

cycle of life begins again.

Epilogue

I AM A ROMAN CATHOLIC priest, and I live and work in Brooklyn, New York. A few years ago, partly because I like to cook, partly because I am of Sicilian origin, I decided to spend my vacation at the Regaleali cooking school in central Sicily. I knew I would meet Anna Tasca Lanza and the rest of the Tasca family and taste their famous wines and that I would be studying under Mario Lo Menzo, one of the last of the *monzù* chefs. What I didn't know about was the sheep.

Sheep play a very important role in life at Regaleali. Every day their milk is transformed into delicious cheeses by Toto Di Martino, the head shepherd, and their meat is made into fabulous lamb dishes by Mario.

My room at Regaleali was near the sheepfold, and early in the morning when the shepherds took the sheep out to pasture, I was awakened by the musical sound of their bleating and the ringing of their bells. Soon I began to walk with the shepherds.

I had never met a shepherd before, and it amazed me that these old men, their faces rugged and worn from the sun and wind, had spent their entire lives tending sheep. As we walked together, they told me stories about the sheep, how this one was too slow, how that one had a bad temper, how another had hurt its leg. From time to time, they would yell out to a sheep that was wandering off, and it would return immediately to the fold. At other times, they would use the most colorful Sicilian curses imaginable to calm down an animal that was acting wild.

When it was time to milk the ewes, the shepherds rounded them up and pushed them, one by one, to the sheepgate. As each came forward, the shepherds would talk to it, scolding it for misbehaving that day or cajoling it to give more milk. It fascinated me that the shepherds could tell the sheep apart—they all looked alike to me—and how they talked to the sheep like a father to his children.

Suddenly the words of the New Testament came back to me. "I am the Good Shepherd. I know My sheep and they know Me." And "I am the Sheepgate, no one can go to the Father but through Me." And "I have other sheep who are not of this fold. These do not know My voice."

In all the years of my life as a priest, I had used those texts in my sermons, speaking out of faith, not knowledge. Now, for the first time, I had the chance to see, hear, smell, and touch real sheep and real shepherds. I began to study them to learn what I could to help me as a shepherd of souls, a pastor. I saw how the shepherds loved and guided their flock and how they cared for the sheep that had gone astray.

No matter what else happened at Regaleali during the day, I could not get the thought of the sheep out of my mind. God was very present at Regaleali that week, and He had His own lessons to give.

Now that I am back in Brooklyn, I tell my flock about what I saw at Regaleali, and I remind them of the words of our Lord: "Blessed are they that have not seen and yet have believed."

Reverend Ronald T. Marino
Brooklyn, New York

Acknowledgments

I NEVER THOUGHT I WOULD enjoy working on this book as much as I did. I made new friends, real friends, the kind you can count on. I am speaking of Susan Derecskey and Ann Yonkers in Washington, D.C. For two years they were with me almost every day in person or by fax. Ours was a collaborative journey of high stakes and high emotions bringing Sicily to the United States.

Susan pulled the book together and helped me write it in a language not my own. She understood my moods and thoughts from the start, sometimes even before I knew them myself.

Ann cooked Sicilian with me and with Mario both at Regaleali and in Washington, D.C. The fact that she and I became great friends speaks volumes about our shared passion for this wonderful food and our mutual resolve to get it right.

Two other Americans whose help has been invaluable are Mary Simeti and Faith Willinger, who live in Italy. Mary has encouraged me in this adventure from the beginning and given me the benefit of her wonderful critical sense. Faith is always generous with her advice; I turn to her when I need it, and she has never failed me. I call Susan, Ann, Mary, and Faith my four American Pillars, after the name of a rose that grows in my garden at Regaleali. I could not have done this book without them.

Another person who has been at my side all along the way is Father Ronald Marino. Ever since he visited Regaleali in the early days of the cooking school, he has acted as my agent in New York. I feel I can always rely on him for assistance and comfort.

My gratitude also goes to Judith Weber, my literary agent, and Roy Finamore, my editor, both of whom believed in me and the book at first sight.

In Sicily, I was lucky to find Franco Zecchin, the photographer, whose fine eye and feeling for Regaleali contributed to making it come alive on the page.

I sought—and got—answers to my questions concerning agriculture from Vincenzo Curcio, director of agriculture at Regaleali and a close friend of the entire family, and Giovanni Carpinello, our neighbor, who has lived in the country most of his life and loves it as much as I do. I would like to express my appreciation to both of them.

I would like to thank Vences, my husband, for his patience and for his advice on the matters that interest him most, history and language.

I can never thank my family enough—my parents, my brother and sisters, my daughter and her husband—for their love.

Above all, I want to thank all the people who work at Regaleali and keep it beautiful. In one way or another, each of them has made me want to write this book and make it a success.

Index

An *italic* page number indicates a page on which a photograph appears.

251

Conversions

Equivalent Imperial and Metric Measurements

American cooks use standard containers, the 8-ounce cup and a tablespoon that takes exactly 16 level fillings to fill that cup level. Measuring by cup makes it very difficult to give weight equivalents, as a cup of densely packed butter will weigh considerably more than a cup of flour. The easiest way therefore to deal with cup measurements in recipes is to take the amount by volume rather than by weight. Thus the equation reads:

1 cup = 240 ml = 8 fl. oz.　　½ cup = 120 ml = 4 fl. oz.

It is possible to buy a set of American cup measures in major stores around the world.

In the States, butter is often measured in sticks. One stick is the equivalent of 8 tablespoons. One tablespoon of butter is therefore the equivalent to ½ ounce/14 grams.

Liquid Measures

Fluid ounces	U.S. measures	Imperial measures	Milliliters
	1 TSP	1 TSP	5
	2 TSP	1 DESSERTSPOON	10
½	1 TBS	1 TBS	14
1	2 TBS	2 TBS	28
2	¼ CUP	4 TBS	56
4	½ CUP		110
5		¼ PINT OR 1 GILL	140
6	¾ CUP		170
8	1 CUP		225
9			250 OR ¼ LITER
10	1 ¼ CUPS	½ PINT	280
12	1 ½ CUPS		340
15		¾ PINT	420
16	2 CUPS		450
18	2 ¼ CUPS		500 OR ½ LITER
20	2 ½ CUPS	1 PINT	560
24	3 CUPS		675
25		1 ¼ PINTS	700
27	3 ½ CUPS		750
30	3 ¾ CUPS	1 ½ PINTS	840
32	4 CUPS OR 1 QUART		900
35		1 ¾ PINTS	980
36	4 ½ CUPS		1000 OR 1 LITER
40	5 CUPS	2 PINTS OR 1 QUART	1120
48	6 CUPS		1350
50		2 ½ PINTS	1400
60	7 ½ CUPS	3 PINTS	1680
64	8 CUPS OR 2 QUARTS		1800
72	9 CUPS		2000 OR 2 LITERS
80	10 CUPS	4 PINTS	2250
96	12 CUPS OR 3 QUARTS		2700
100		5 PINTS	2800

Solid Measures

U.S. and Imperial Measures		Metric Measures	
OUNCES	POUNDS	GRAMS	KILOS
1		28	
2		56	
3½		100	
4	¼	112	
5		140	
6		168	
8	½	225	
9		250	¼
12	¾	340	
16	1	450	
18		500	½
20	1¼	560	
24	1½	675	
27		750	¾
28	1¾	780	
32	2	900	
36	2¼	1000	1
40	2½	1100	
48	3	1350	
54		1500	1½
64	4	1800	
72	4½	2000	2
80	5	2250	2¼
90		2500	2½
100	6	2800	2¼

Suggested Equivalents and Substitutes for Ingredients

all-purpose flour—plain flour
arugula—rocket
beet—beetroot
bell peppers—fleshy peppers
bouillon cubes—stock cubes
coarse salt—kitchen salt
confectioners' sugar—icing sugar
cornstarch—cornflour
eggplant—aubergine
fava beans—broad beans
flat-leaf parsley—continental parsley
granulated sugar—caster sugar
green grapes—white grapes
romaine—cos lettuce
scallion—spring onion
sour cherry—morello cherry
squash—courgettes or marrow
tomato paste—tomato concentrate
unbleached flour—strong, white flour
vanilla bean—vanilla pod
zest—rind
zucchini—courgettes
heavy cream—double cream
baking sheet—oven tray
cheesecloth—muslin
parchment paper—greaseproof paper
plastic wrap—cling film

Oven Temperature Equivalents

Fahrenheit	Celsius	Gas Mark	Description
225	110	¼	Cool
250	130	½	
275	140	1	Very Slow
300	150	2	
325	170	3	Slow
350	180	4	Moderate
375	190	5	
400	200	6	Moderately Hot
425	220	7	Fairly Hot
450	230	8	Hot
475	240	9	Very Hot
500	250	10	Extremely Hot

Any broiling recipes can be used with the grill of the oven, but beware of high-temperature grills.